50 Budget Bite Recipes for Home

By: Kelly Johnson

Table of Contents

- Spaghetti Aglio e Olio
- Vegetarian Chili
- Garlic Parmesan Roasted Cauliflower
- Stuffed Bell Peppers
- Quinoa Salad
- One-Pot Chicken and Rice
- Bean and Cheese Burritos
- Pasta Primavera
- Black Bean Soup
- Caprese Salad
- Mushroom Risotto
- Sweet Potato and Black Bean Tacos
- Greek Salad
- Tomato Basil Soup
- Vegetable Stir-Fry
- Tuna Salad
- Pesto Pasta
- Broccoli Cheddar Soup
- Eggplant Parmesan
- Cucumber Avocado Salad
- Lentil Soup
- Chicken Quesadillas
- Pineapple Fried Rice
- Cabbage Stir-Fry
- Sausage and Peppers
- Mango Salsa
- Spinach and Feta Stuffed Chicken
- Ratatouille
- Cilantro Lime Rice
- Chickpea Curry
- Bruschetta
- Zucchini Noodles with Marinara
- Stuffed Mushrooms
- Corn and Black Bean Salad
- Lemon Garlic Shrimp
- Potato Leek Soup

- BBQ Chicken Drumsticks
- Cauliflower Rice Stir-Fry
- Italian Sausage Pasta
- Hummus and Veggie Wraps
- Teriyaki Tofu
- Broccoli Salad
- Pulled Pork Sandwiches
- Pasta with Garlic Butter Sauce
- Quiche
- Asian Slaw
- Baked Salmon
- Rice and Beans
- Stuffed Zucchini Boats
- Avocado Toast

Spaghetti Aglio e Olio

Ingredients:

- 1/2 pound (about 225g) spaghetti
- 1/3 cup extra virgin olive oil
- 4-6 cloves garlic, thinly sliced
- 1/2 teaspoon red pepper flakes (adjust to taste)
- Salt, to taste
- Freshly ground black pepper, to taste
- Fresh parsley, chopped, for garnish
- Grated Parmesan cheese, for serving (optional)

Instructions:

1. **Cook the spaghetti:**
   - Bring a large pot of salted water to a boil. Cook the spaghetti according to package instructions until al dente. Reserve about 1 cup of pasta water before draining.
2. **Prepare the sauce:**
   - While the pasta is cooking, heat the olive oil in a large skillet over medium heat.
   - Add the thinly sliced garlic and red pepper flakes. Cook, stirring frequently, until the garlic is golden brown and fragrant, about 1-2 minutes. Be careful not to burn the garlic.
3. **Combine pasta and sauce:**
   - Add the cooked spaghetti directly to the skillet with the garlic and oil. Toss well to coat the pasta evenly with the garlic-infused olive oil.
4. **Adjust seasoning and consistency:**
   - Season with salt and freshly ground black pepper to taste. If the pasta seems dry, add a splash of the reserved pasta water to loosen the sauce and help it coat the spaghetti.
5. **Serve:**
   - Transfer the spaghetti aglio e olio to serving plates or bowls.
   - Garnish with chopped fresh parsley and grated Parmesan cheese, if desired.
6. **Enjoy:**
   - Serve immediately while hot and enjoy the simple and delicious flavors of spaghetti aglio e olio!

This dish is perfect for a quick and satisfying meal, showcasing the natural flavors of garlic and olive oil with a hint of spice from the red pepper flakes. Adjust the seasoning and spice level to suit your preferences, and pair it with a fresh salad or crusty bread for a complete meal.

Garlic Parmesan Roasted Cauliflower

Ingredients:

- 1 large head of cauliflower, cut into florets
- 3 tablespoons olive oil
- 4 cloves garlic, minced
- 1/2 cup grated Parmesan cheese
- 1 teaspoon Italian seasoning (or a mix of dried oregano, basil, and thyme)
- Salt and pepper, to taste
- Fresh parsley, chopped, for garnish (optional)

Instructions:

1. **Preheat the oven** to 425°F (220°C). Line a baking sheet with parchment paper or foil for easy cleanup.
2. **Prepare the cauliflower:**
    - Cut the cauliflower into florets of similar size. Place them in a large bowl.
3. **Make the garlic Parmesan mixture:**
    - In a small bowl, combine the olive oil, minced garlic, grated Parmesan cheese, and Italian seasoning. Stir well to mix.
4. **Coat the cauliflower:**
    - Pour the garlic Parmesan mixture over the cauliflower florets. Use your hands or a spoon to toss and coat the cauliflower evenly with the mixture.
5. **Season:**
    - Season the cauliflower with salt and pepper to taste. Adjust the seasoning according to your preference.
6. **Roast the cauliflower:**
    - Spread the cauliflower florets in a single layer on the prepared baking sheet.
    - Roast in the preheated oven for 20-25 minutes, or until the cauliflower is tender and golden brown, tossing halfway through cooking for even browning.
7. **Serve:**
    - Remove from the oven and transfer the roasted cauliflower to a serving dish.
    - Garnish with chopped fresh parsley if desired.
8. **Enjoy:**
    - Serve the garlic Parmesan roasted cauliflower as a delicious side dish alongside your favorite main course. It's perfect for a family dinner or as a tasty addition to a holiday meal.

This dish is versatile and can be adjusted to suit your taste preferences. You can also add a squeeze of lemon juice or sprinkle with red pepper flakes for added flavor variation.

Stuffed Bell Peppers

Ingredients:

- 4 large bell peppers (any color)
- 1 pound ground beef (or turkey, chicken, or a vegetarian alternative)
- 1 cup cooked rice (white or brown)
- 1 can (14 ounces) diced tomatoes, drained
- 1 cup shredded cheese (cheddar, mozzarella, or your favorite)
- 1/2 cup onion, finely chopped
- 2 cloves garlic, minced
- 1 teaspoon dried oregano
- 1 teaspoon dried basil
- Salt and pepper, to taste
- Fresh parsley or basil, chopped, for garnish (optional)

Instructions:

1. **Prepare the bell peppers:**
    - Preheat your oven to 375°F (190°C). Grease a baking dish large enough to hold the bell peppers upright.
    - Cut the tops off the bell peppers and remove the seeds and membranes. If needed, trim the bottoms slightly so they stand upright in the baking dish.
2. **Prepare the filling:**
    - In a large skillet, cook the ground beef (or other protein) over medium-high heat until browned and cooked through. Drain any excess fat.
    - Add the chopped onion and minced garlic to the skillet. Cook for 2-3 minutes, until the onion is softened and translucent.
    - Stir in the cooked rice, diced tomatoes, dried oregano, dried basil, salt, and pepper. Cook for another 2-3 minutes to blend the flavors.
3. **Stuff the bell peppers:**
    - Spoon the filling mixture into each bell pepper until they are full and slightly heaping. Press the filling down gently with the back of the spoon.
4. **Bake the stuffed peppers:**
    - Place the stuffed bell peppers upright in the prepared baking dish.
    - Cover the baking dish with foil and bake in the preheated oven for 30-35 minutes, or until the peppers are tender.
5. **Add cheese and finish baking:**
    - Remove the foil from the baking dish and sprinkle the shredded cheese evenly over the tops of the stuffed peppers.
    - Return the baking dish to the oven and bake, uncovered, for an additional 10 minutes or until the cheese is melted and bubbly.
6. **Serve:**
    - Remove the stuffed bell peppers from the oven and let them cool slightly.
    - Garnish with chopped fresh parsley or basil, if desired, before serving.

7. **Enjoy:**
    - Serve the stuffed bell peppers hot as a delicious and hearty meal. They pair well with a side salad or crusty bread.

These stuffed bell peppers are versatile, and you can customize the filling with your favorite ingredients such as beans, quinoa, or different types of cheeses. They are great for meal prep and can be stored in the refrigerator for a few days for easy reheating.

Quinoa Salad

Ingredients:

- 1 cup quinoa
- 2 cups water or vegetable broth
- 1 can (15 ounces) chickpeas, drained and rinsed
- 1 cup cherry tomatoes, halved
- 1 cucumber, diced
- 1/2 red bell pepper, diced
- 1/4 cup red onion, finely chopped
- 1/4 cup fresh parsley, chopped
- 1/4 cup fresh mint, chopped (optional)
- Juice of 1 lemon (about 2-3 tablespoons)
- 3 tablespoons extra virgin olive oil
- 1 clove garlic, minced
- Salt and pepper, to taste

Instructions:

1. **Rinse and cook the quinoa:**
   - Rinse the quinoa under cold water using a fine mesh sieve to remove any bitterness.
   - In a medium saucepan, bring the water or vegetable broth to a boil. Add the quinoa, reduce heat to low, cover, and simmer for 15-20 minutes, or until the quinoa is cooked and all the liquid is absorbed. Remove from heat and let it sit, covered, for 5 minutes. Fluff with a fork and let it cool.
2. **Prepare the dressing:**
   - In a small bowl, whisk together the lemon juice, olive oil, minced garlic, salt, and pepper to make the dressing. Adjust seasoning to taste.
3. **Assemble the salad:**
   - In a large mixing bowl, combine the cooked and cooled quinoa with the chickpeas, cherry tomatoes, cucumber, red bell pepper, red onion, parsley, and mint (if using).
   - Pour the dressing over the salad and toss gently to combine, ensuring the ingredients are evenly coated with the dressing.
4. **Chill and serve:**
   - Cover the quinoa salad and refrigerate for at least 30 minutes to allow the flavors to meld together.
   - Serve chilled as a refreshing salad option for lunch or dinner.
5. **Enjoy:**
   - Garnish with additional chopped herbs or a sprinkle of feta cheese if desired, and enjoy this nutritious and flavorful quinoa salad!

This quinoa salad is packed with protein, fiber, and fresh vegetables, making it a healthy and satisfying meal. It can be customized with your favorite ingredients such as avocado, olives, or grilled chicken for added variety and flavor.

One-Pot Chicken and Rice

Ingredients:

- 1 tablespoon olive oil
- 4 boneless, skinless chicken thighs (or breasts), cut into bite-sized pieces
- 1 onion, diced
- 2 cloves garlic, minced
- 1 cup long-grain white rice
- 2 cups chicken broth
- 1 cup diced tomatoes (fresh or canned)
- 1 teaspoon dried thyme
- 1 teaspoon paprika
- Salt and pepper, to taste
- 1 cup frozen peas (optional)
- Fresh parsley, chopped, for garnish

Instructions:

1. **Sear the chicken:**
   - In a large pot or deep skillet, heat the olive oil over medium-high heat. Add the chicken pieces and cook until browned on all sides, about 4-5 minutes. Remove the chicken from the pot and set aside.
2. **Cook the aromatics:**
   - In the same pot, add the diced onion and cook for 3-4 minutes until softened. Add the minced garlic and cook for another 1-2 minutes until fragrant.
3. **Add rice and liquids:**
   - Stir in the rice, chicken broth, diced tomatoes (with juices), dried thyme, paprika, salt, and pepper. Bring to a boil.
4. **Simmer:**
   - Reduce the heat to low, cover the pot with a lid, and simmer for 15-20 minutes, or until the rice is tender and has absorbed the liquid. Stir occasionally to prevent sticking.
5. **Add chicken and peas:**
   - Stir in the cooked chicken pieces and frozen peas (if using). Cover and cook for an additional 5-7 minutes, or until the chicken is cooked through and the peas are heated through.
6. **Serve:**
   - Remove from heat and let it sit covered for a few minutes.
   - Fluff the chicken and rice mixture with a fork. Adjust seasoning with salt and pepper if needed.
7. **Garnish and serve:**
   - Sprinkle with chopped fresh parsley before serving.
8. **Enjoy:**

- Serve the one-pot chicken and rice hot, straight from the pot. It's a complete meal with protein, grains, and vegetables all cooked together for a delicious and hearty dish.

This one-pot chicken and rice recipe is versatile, and you can customize it by adding your favorite vegetables or herbs. It's perfect for a family dinner or meal prepping for the week ahead.

Bean and Cheese Burritos

Ingredients:

- 1 can (15 ounces) refried beans
- 1 cup shredded cheese (cheddar, Monterey Jack, or a blend)
- 4 large flour tortillas (10-inch diameter)
- 1/2 cup salsa (optional)
- 1/4 cup sour cream (optional)
- Fresh cilantro, chopped (optional)
- Salt and pepper, to taste

Instructions:

1. **Prepare the filling:**
    - In a microwave-safe bowl, heat the refried beans until warm. Stir in salt and pepper to taste.
2. **Assemble the burritos:**
    - Lay out the flour tortillas on a clean surface.
    - Spread an equal amount of warm refried beans onto each tortilla, leaving a border around the edges.
    - Sprinkle shredded cheese evenly over the beans.
3. **Roll the burritos:**
    - Fold the sides of each tortilla over the filling, then roll it up tightly from the bottom to enclose the filling completely.
4. **Heat the burritos:**
    - Heat a large skillet over medium heat. Place each burrito, seam side down, in the skillet.
    - Cook for 2-3 minutes on each side, or until the tortilla is golden brown and crispy, and the cheese is melted.
5. **Serve:**
    - Remove the burritos from the skillet and place them on a serving plate.
    - Cut each burrito in half diagonally, if desired.
6. **Garnish and enjoy:**
    - Serve the bean and cheese burritos hot with salsa, sour cream, and chopped cilantro on the side, if desired.
    - These burritos are perfect for a quick lunch or dinner. They can also be wrapped individually in foil and stored in the refrigerator for easy reheating later.

Feel free to customize your bean and cheese burritos by adding additional ingredients such as diced tomatoes, avocado slices, or cooked rice. Enjoy this hearty and delicious meal!

Pasta Primavera

Ingredients:

- 12 ounces (340g) pasta (such as fettuccine, linguine, or spaghetti)
- 2 tablespoons olive oil
- 2 cloves garlic, minced
- 1 small onion, thinly sliced
- 1 cup cherry tomatoes, halved
- 1 medium zucchini, sliced into half moons
- 1 medium yellow squash, sliced into half moons
- 1 cup broccoli florets
- 1 cup bell peppers (any color), sliced
- 1/2 cup peas (fresh or frozen)
- Salt and pepper, to taste
- 1 cup heavy cream (or half-and-half for a lighter version)
- 1/2 cup grated Parmesan cheese
- 1/4 cup fresh basil or parsley, chopped, for garnish

Instructions:

1. **Cook the pasta:**
    - Cook the pasta in a large pot of salted boiling water according to package instructions until al dente. Drain and set aside, reserving about 1 cup of pasta cooking water.
2. **Prepare the vegetables:**
    - In a large skillet or pan, heat the olive oil over medium heat. Add the minced garlic and sliced onion. Sauté for 2-3 minutes until fragrant and the onion is translucent.
    - Add the cherry tomatoes, zucchini, yellow squash, broccoli, bell peppers, and peas to the skillet. Cook for 5-7 minutes, stirring occasionally, until the vegetables are tender-crisp. Season with salt and pepper to taste.
3. **Make the sauce:**
    - Pour the heavy cream (or half-and-half) into the skillet with the cooked vegetables. Stir in the grated Parmesan cheese until melted and combined. Cook for 2-3 minutes until the sauce has thickened slightly.
4. **Combine pasta and sauce:**
    - Add the cooked pasta to the skillet with the creamy vegetable sauce. Toss gently to coat the pasta evenly with the sauce. If needed, add a splash of the reserved pasta cooking water to loosen the sauce.
5. **Serve:**
    - Remove from heat and garnish with chopped fresh basil or parsley.
6. **Enjoy:**
    - Serve the Pasta Primavera immediately, garnished with extra grated Parmesan cheese if desired.

Pasta Primavera is a versatile dish, so feel free to customize it with your favorite vegetables or herbs. It's a perfect way to enjoy the flavors of seasonal produce in a creamy and satisfying pasta dish!

Black Bean Soup

Ingredients:

- 2 tablespoons olive oil
- 1 onion, chopped
- 2 cloves garlic, minced
- 2 carrots, diced
- 2 celery stalks, diced
- 1 red bell pepper, diced
- 2 cans (15 ounces each) black beans, drained and rinsed
- 4 cups vegetable broth (or chicken broth)
- 1 can (14.5 ounces) diced tomatoes
- 1 teaspoon ground cumin
- 1 teaspoon chili powder (adjust to taste)
- Salt and pepper, to taste
- Juice of 1 lime (optional)
- Fresh cilantro, chopped, for garnish
- Sour cream or Greek yogurt, for serving (optional)

Instructions:

1. **Sauté the vegetables:**
    - Heat olive oil in a large pot or Dutch oven over medium heat. Add the chopped onion and cook for 3-4 minutes until softened.
    - Add the minced garlic, diced carrots, diced celery, and diced red bell pepper. Cook for another 5 minutes, stirring occasionally, until the vegetables are tender.
2. **Add beans and broth:**
    - Stir in the black beans, vegetable broth (or chicken broth), and diced tomatoes (with juices) into the pot.
3. **Season and simmer:**
    - Add ground cumin, chili powder, salt, and pepper to taste. Stir well to combine.
    - Bring the soup to a boil, then reduce the heat to low. Cover and simmer for 20-25 minutes to allow the flavors to meld together.
4. **Blend (optional):**
    - For a smoother consistency, use an immersion blender to partially blend the soup directly in the pot until desired texture is achieved. Alternatively, transfer a portion of the soup to a blender and blend until smooth, then return it to the pot.
5. **Finish and serve:**
    - Stir in fresh lime juice if using. Taste and adjust seasoning if needed.
    - Ladle the black bean soup into bowls. Garnish with chopped fresh cilantro and a dollop of sour cream or Greek yogurt if desired.
6. **Enjoy:**
    - Serve the black bean soup hot, accompanied by crusty bread or tortilla chips for a delicious and comforting meal.

This black bean soup recipe is versatile and can be adapted based on your preferences. It's packed with protein and fiber, making it a satisfying option for a healthy lunch or dinner.

Caprese Salad

Ingredients:

- 2 large ripe tomatoes, sliced
- 1 ball fresh mozzarella cheese, sliced
- Fresh basil leaves
- Extra virgin olive oil, for drizzling
- Balsamic glaze or balsamic vinegar, for drizzling
- Salt and pepper, to taste

Instructions:

1. **Prepare the ingredients:**
   - Slice the tomatoes and fresh mozzarella cheese into uniform slices, about 1/4 inch thick.
   - Arrange the tomato slices on a serving platter or individual plates.
   - Place a slice of mozzarella cheese on top of each tomato slice.
2. **Assemble the salad:**
   - Tuck fresh basil leaves between the tomato and mozzarella slices. You can use whole leaves or chiffonade (thinly sliced) basil.
3. **Season:**
   - Season the Caprese salad with salt and freshly ground black pepper, to taste.
4. **Drizzle with olive oil and balsamic glaze:**
   - Drizzle extra virgin olive oil over the tomato and mozzarella slices.
   - Follow with a drizzle of balsamic glaze or balsamic vinegar for added sweetness and flavor.
5. **Garnish and serve:**
   - Garnish the Caprese salad with additional fresh basil leaves if desired.
6. **Enjoy:**
   - Serve the Caprese salad immediately as an appetizer or side dish. It pairs beautifully with crusty bread or as a light accompaniment to grilled meats.

Caprese salad is best enjoyed when tomatoes and basil are in season for the freshest flavors. It's a simple and elegant dish that showcases the wonderful combination of fresh ingredients and Mediterranean flavors.

Mushroom Risotto

Ingredients:

- 1 cup Arborio rice
- 4 cups vegetable or chicken broth
- 2 tablespoons olive oil
- 2 tablespoons unsalted butter
- 1 onion, finely chopped
- 2 cloves garlic, minced
- 8 ounces (225g) mushrooms (such as cremini, button, or wild mushrooms), sliced
- 1/2 cup dry white wine (optional)
- 1/2 cup grated Parmesan cheese
- Salt and pepper, to taste
- Fresh parsley, chopped, for garnish

Instructions:

1. **Prepare the broth:**
   - In a saucepan, heat the vegetable or chicken broth over medium heat. Bring to a simmer and keep warm.
2. **Sauté the mushrooms:**
   - In a large, deep skillet or Dutch oven, heat 1 tablespoon of olive oil over medium heat. Add the sliced mushrooms and cook until they are golden brown and tender, about 5-7 minutes. Season with salt and pepper. Remove the mushrooms from the skillet and set aside.
3. **Cook the aromatics:**
   - In the same skillet, add the remaining tablespoon of olive oil and 1 tablespoon of butter. Add the chopped onion and cook until softened, about 3-4 minutes. Add the minced garlic and cook for another 1 minute until fragrant.
4. **Toast the rice:**
   - Add the Arborio rice to the skillet with the onions and garlic. Stir to coat the rice with the oil and cook for 1-2 minutes until the rice becomes translucent around the edges.
5. **Deglaze with wine (if using):**
   - Pour in the white wine and stir continuously until it is absorbed by the rice.
6. **Add the broth:**
   - Begin adding the warm broth to the rice mixture, one ladleful (about 1/2 cup) at a time, stirring frequently. Allow each addition of broth to be absorbed by the rice before adding more. This process helps to release the starch from the rice and create a creamy texture.
   - Continue adding broth and stirring until the rice is creamy and tender, but still slightly firm to the bite (al dente). This typically takes about 18-20 minutes.
7. **Finish the risotto:**

- - Stir in the cooked mushrooms and remaining tablespoon of butter into the risotto until well combined.
  - Stir in the grated Parmesan cheese until melted and incorporated into the risotto. Season with salt and pepper to taste.
8. **Serve:**
   - Remove the skillet from heat. Garnish the mushroom risotto with chopped fresh parsley.
9. **Enjoy:**
   - Serve the mushroom risotto immediately while hot, as a main dish or alongside grilled meats or vegetables.

This mushroom risotto recipe yields a creamy and comforting dish with rich flavors from the mushrooms and Parmesan cheese. It's perfect for a cozy dinner at home or as an impressive dish for guests.

Sweet Potato and Black Bean Tacos

Ingredients:

- 2 medium sweet potatoes, peeled and diced into small cubes
- 1 tablespoon olive oil
- 1 teaspoon ground cumin
- 1 teaspoon chili powder
- Salt and pepper, to taste
- 1 can (15 ounces) black beans, drained and rinsed
- 1/2 cup corn kernels (fresh, canned, or frozen)
- 1/2 red onion, finely chopped
- 1/4 cup fresh cilantro, chopped
- Juice of 1 lime
- 8 small corn or flour tortillas
- Optional toppings: avocado slices, salsa, sour cream or Greek yogurt, shredded cheese, hot sauce

Instructions:

1. **Roast the sweet potatoes:**
    - Preheat the oven to 400°F (200°C). Place the diced sweet potatoes on a baking sheet. Drizzle with olive oil and sprinkle with ground cumin, chili powder, salt, and pepper. Toss to coat evenly.
    - Roast in the preheated oven for 20-25 minutes, or until the sweet potatoes are tender and lightly caramelized, stirring halfway through.
2. **Prepare the black bean mixture:**
    - In a medium skillet, heat a drizzle of olive oil over medium heat. Add the chopped red onion and cook for 3-4 minutes until softened.
    - Add the black beans and corn kernels to the skillet. Cook for 5-7 minutes, stirring occasionally, until heated through.
3. **Combine and season:**
    - Transfer the roasted sweet potatoes to the skillet with the black bean mixture.
    - Add chopped cilantro and squeeze fresh lime juice over the mixture. Stir well to combine. Taste and adjust seasoning with salt and pepper if needed.
4. **Warm the tortillas:**
    - Heat the tortillas in a dry skillet or microwave until warm and pliable.
5. **Assemble the tacos:**
    - Spoon the sweet potato and black bean mixture onto each tortilla.
    - Add optional toppings such as avocado slices, salsa, sour cream or Greek yogurt, shredded cheese, and hot sauce according to your preference.
6. **Serve:**
    - Serve the sweet potato and black bean tacos immediately, garnished with additional cilantro and lime wedges on the side.

These sweet potato and black bean tacos are packed with flavor, nutrients, and are perfect for a quick and satisfying meal. They can be easily customized with different toppings and enjoyed any time of the year!

Greek Salad

Ingredients:

- 3 medium tomatoes, cut into wedges
- 1 cucumber, sliced
- 1 red onion, thinly sliced
- 1 green bell pepper, seeded and sliced
- 1/2 cup Kalamata olives
- 1/2 cup crumbled feta cheese
- Fresh oregano leaves or dried oregano (optional), for garnish

For the dressing:

- 1/4 cup extra virgin olive oil
- 2 tablespoons red wine vinegar
- 1 clove garlic, minced
- 1 teaspoon dried oregano
- Salt and pepper, to taste

Instructions:

1. **Prepare the vegetables:**
   - In a large salad bowl, combine the tomato wedges, sliced cucumber, thinly sliced red onion, and sliced green bell pepper.
2. **Add olives and feta:**
   - Add the Kalamata olives and crumbled feta cheese to the bowl.
3. **Make the dressing:**
   - In a small bowl, whisk together the extra virgin olive oil, red wine vinegar, minced garlic, dried oregano, salt, and pepper.
4. **Dress the salad:**
   - Pour the dressing over the salad ingredients in the bowl.
5. **Toss gently:**
   - Gently toss all the ingredients together until evenly coated with the dressing.
6. **Garnish and serve:**
   - Garnish the Greek salad with fresh oregano leaves or a sprinkle of dried oregano for extra flavor.
7. **Enjoy:**
   - Serve the Greek salad immediately as a refreshing side dish or light meal.

This Greek salad recipe is versatile and can be customized with additional ingredients such as cherry tomatoes, pepperoncini peppers, or even a sprinkle of capers. It's perfect for summer gatherings or as a healthy addition to any meal!

Tomato Basil Soup

Ingredients:

- 1 tablespoon olive oil
- 1 onion, chopped
- 2 cloves garlic, minced
- 2 cans (28 ounces each) whole tomatoes
- 1 cup vegetable broth (or chicken broth)
- 1 teaspoon sugar (optional, to balance acidity)
- Salt and pepper to taste
- 1/2 cup fresh basil leaves, chopped (plus more for garnish)
- 1/2 cup heavy cream (optional, for a creamier texture)

Instructions:

1. **Sauté onions and garlic**: In a large pot, heat the olive oil over medium heat. Add the chopped onion and cook until softened, about 5 minutes. Add the minced garlic and cook for another 1-2 minutes until fragrant.
2. **Simmer tomatoes**: Add the canned tomatoes (including juices) to the pot. Use a spoon to break up the tomatoes into smaller pieces.
3. **Add broth and season**: Pour in the vegetable broth (or chicken broth). Add sugar if using, then season with salt and pepper to taste.
4. **Simmer**: Bring the soup to a boil, then reduce the heat and let it simmer for about 15-20 minutes, stirring occasionally.
5. **Blend**: Remove the pot from heat. Using an immersion blender, blend the soup until smooth. (Alternatively, you can carefully transfer the soup in batches to a blender and blend until smooth, then return to the pot.)
6. **Add basil and cream**: Stir in the chopped basil leaves. If using heavy cream, add it at this stage for a creamier soup.
7. **Serve**: Ladle the soup into bowls. Garnish with additional chopped basil leaves if desired. Serve hot with crusty bread or a side salad.

Enjoy your homemade Tomato Basil Soup! It's perfect for a cozy lunch or dinner, especially on a chilly day.

Vegetable Stir-Fry

Ingredients:

- 2 tablespoons vegetable oil (such as peanut, sesame, or canola oil)
- 1 onion, sliced
- 2 cloves garlic, minced
- 1-inch piece of ginger, minced or grated
- Assorted vegetables, such as:
    - 1 bell pepper, sliced
    - 1 carrot, julienned or thinly sliced
    - 1 zucchini, sliced
    - 1 cup broccoli florets
    - 1 cup snap peas or snow peas
- Salt and pepper, to taste
- Soy sauce or tamari, to taste
- Optional toppings: sesame seeds, chopped green onions, crushed red pepper flakes

Instructions:

1. **Prepare vegetables**: Wash and cut all vegetables into bite-sized pieces or thin slices.
2. **Heat oil**: Heat vegetable oil in a large skillet or wok over medium-high heat.
3. **Sauté aromatics**: Add sliced onion and sauté for 2-3 minutes until softened. Add minced garlic and ginger, stir-fry for another minute until fragrant.
4. **Add vegetables**: Start with the vegetables that take longer to cook, such as carrots and broccoli. Stir-fry for 3-4 minutes until they begin to soften slightly.
5. **Cook remaining vegetables**: Add bell peppers, zucchini, snap peas, or any other quick-cooking vegetables. Stir-fry for another 2-3 minutes until all vegetables are tender-crisp. Be careful not to overcook—they should remain colorful and slightly crisp.
6. **Season**: Season with salt, pepper, and soy sauce or tamari to taste. Adjust seasoning as needed.
7. **Finish**: Remove from heat. Optionally, sprinkle with sesame seeds, chopped green onions, or crushed red pepper flakes for added flavor and garnish.
8. **Serve**: Serve the vegetable stir-fry immediately while hot, either as a main dish or alongside rice or noodles.

Tips:

- **Preparation**: Ensure all vegetables are cut uniformly to ensure even cooking.
- **Heat control**: Keep the heat high enough to stir-fry quickly but not so high that the vegetables burn.
- **Variations**: Feel free to add protein such as tofu, chicken, shrimp, or beef to make it a more substantial meal.

- **Sauce**: If you prefer a saucier stir-fry, you can mix soy sauce or tamari with a bit of cornstarch and water to thicken.

Enjoy your homemade vegetable stir-fry! It's a nutritious and flavorful dish that's perfect for a quick and healthy meal.

Tuna Salad

Ingredients:

- 2 cans (5 ounces each) of tuna, drained
- 1/2 cup mayonnaise (adjust amount based on preference)
- 1 tablespoon Dijon mustard (optional, for added flavor)
- 1 celery stalk, finely chopped
- 1/4 cup red onion, finely chopped (or substitute with green onions/scallions)
- 1 tablespoon fresh lemon juice
- Salt and pepper, to taste
- Optional add-ins: chopped pickles, capers, chopped parsley, diced apples, or grapes

Instructions:

1. **Prepare tuna**: Drain the tuna thoroughly and transfer it to a mixing bowl.
2. **Mix dressing**: In a small bowl, combine mayonnaise, Dijon mustard (if using), and fresh lemon juice. Mix until well combined.
3. **Combine ingredients**: Add the chopped celery, red onion (or green onions/scallions), and any optional add-ins you prefer to the tuna in the mixing bowl.
4. **Add dressing**: Pour the mayonnaise mixture over the tuna and vegetables. Gently toss everything together until the tuna is evenly coated with the dressing.
5. **Season**: Taste and season with salt and pepper according to your preference. Adjust lemon juice or additional seasonings if desired.
6. **Chill**: Cover the bowl with plastic wrap or transfer the tuna salad to an airtight container. Refrigerate for at least 30 minutes to allow the flavors to meld.
7. **Serve**: Serve the tuna salad on its own as a side dish, as a sandwich filling between slices of bread or in a wrap, or on a bed of lettuce as a salad.

Tips:

- **Variations**: You can customize your tuna salad by adding different herbs (like dill or parsley), spices (like paprika or cayenne pepper), or additional vegetables (like diced bell peppers or grated carrots).
- **Texture**: If you prefer a chunkier texture, break up the tuna into larger pieces. For a smoother texture, flake the tuna finely with a fork.
- **Storage**: Store leftover tuna salad in an airtight container in the refrigerator for up to 3 days.

This tuna salad recipe is versatile and can be adjusted to suit your taste preferences. It's perfect for a quick lunch, a picnic, or even as a party appetizer. Enjoy!

Pesto Pasta

Ingredients:

- 8 ounces (about 225 grams) of pasta (such as spaghetti, linguine, or penne)
- 2 cups fresh basil leaves, packed
- 1/2 cup grated Parmesan cheese
- 1/3 cup pine nuts (you can also use walnuts or almonds)
- 2 garlic cloves, peeled
- 1/2 cup extra virgin olive oil
- Salt and pepper, to taste
- Optional: cherry tomatoes, diced chicken breast, or grilled vegetables for additional toppings

Instructions:

1. **Cook the pasta**: Bring a large pot of salted water to a boil. Cook the pasta according to the package instructions until al dente. Reserve about 1/2 cup of pasta cooking water before draining.
2. **Make the pesto**: While the pasta is cooking, prepare the pesto. In a food processor or blender, combine the basil leaves, grated Parmesan cheese, pine nuts, and garlic cloves. Pulse until finely chopped.
3. **Add olive oil**: With the food processor running, slowly drizzle in the olive oil until the pesto reaches a smooth consistency. You may need to stop and scrape down the sides of the processor with a spatula.
4. **Season**: Taste the pesto and season with salt and pepper to your liking. Blend again briefly to incorporate the seasoning.
5. **Combine pesto and pasta**: In a large bowl, toss the cooked and drained pasta with the pesto sauce until well coated. If the pasta seems dry, add a bit of the reserved pasta cooking water to loosen the sauce.
6. **Optional toppings**: Add cherry tomatoes, diced chicken breast, grilled vegetables, or any other toppings you desire. Toss gently to combine.
7. **Serve**: Divide the pesto pasta into serving bowls. Optionally, sprinkle with extra Parmesan cheese and garnish with fresh basil leaves.

Tips:

- **Pesto variations**: You can customize your pesto by adding ingredients like spinach, arugula, or parsley for added flavor and color.
- **Texture**: For a chunkier pesto, pulse the ingredients less in the food processor. For a smoother consistency, blend longer.
- **Storage**: Store any leftover pesto in an airtight container in the refrigerator for up to a week. It can also be frozen for longer storage.

Pesto pasta is a delicious and versatile dish that can be enjoyed as a main course or as a side dish. It's perfect for a quick weeknight dinner or for entertaining guests. Enjoy your homemade pesto pasta!

Broccoli Cheddar Soup

Ingredients:

- 4 tablespoons unsalted butter
- 1 onion, chopped
- 2 cloves garlic, minced
- 1/4 cup all-purpose flour
- 4 cups low-sodium chicken or vegetable broth
- 4 cups broccoli florets (about 2 medium heads)
- 1 large carrot, peeled and grated
- 2 cups shredded sharp cheddar cheese
- 1 cup half-and-half or heavy cream
- Salt and pepper, to taste
- Optional: pinch of nutmeg or cayenne pepper for added flavor

Instructions:

1. **Sauté onions and garlic**: In a large pot or Dutch oven, melt the butter over medium heat. Add the chopped onion and cook until softened, about 5 minutes. Add the minced garlic and cook for another 1-2 minutes until fragrant.
2. **Add flour**: Sprinkle the flour over the onion and garlic mixture. Stir constantly for 1-2 minutes to cook the flour, creating a roux.
3. **Simmer**: Gradually whisk in the chicken or vegetable broth, ensuring there are no lumps from the flour. Bring to a boil, then reduce the heat to medium-low.
4. **Add broccoli and carrot**: Add the broccoli florets and grated carrot to the pot. Simmer for about 15-20 minutes until the broccoli is tender.
5. **Blend soup (optional)**: If you prefer a smoother soup, use an immersion blender to blend the soup until it reaches your desired consistency. Alternatively, transfer a portion of the soup to a blender and blend until smooth, then return it to the pot.
6. **Add cheese and cream**: Stir in the shredded cheddar cheese until melted and smooth. Pour in the half-and-half or heavy cream, stirring constantly until the soup is heated through.
7. **Season**: Season with salt and pepper to taste. Add a pinch of nutmeg or cayenne pepper for additional flavor if desired.
8. **Serve**: Ladle the broccoli cheddar soup into bowls. Optionally, garnish with additional shredded cheddar cheese or chopped fresh herbs.

Tips:

- **Texture**: If you prefer a chunkier soup, you can blend only a portion of the soup and leave some broccoli florets intact.

- **Storage**: Store leftovers in an airtight container in the refrigerator for up to 3 days. Reheat gently on the stovetop, adding a splash of broth or cream if needed to thin out the soup.
- **Variations**: You can add diced potatoes or cauliflower along with the broccoli for added texture and flavor variation.

This broccoli cheddar soup recipe is hearty and delicious, perfect for a cozy meal at home. Enjoy!

Eggplant Parmesan

Ingredients:

- 2 large eggplants
- Salt
- 1 cup all-purpose flour
- 3 large eggs, beaten
- 2 cups breadcrumbs (you can use store-bought or make your own)
- 1 cup grated Parmesan cheese
- 2 cups marinara sauce (homemade or store-bought)
- 2 cups shredded mozzarella cheese
- Fresh basil leaves, chopped (for garnish)
- Olive oil, for frying

Instructions:

1. **Prepare the eggplant**: Slice the eggplants into 1/2-inch thick rounds. Place the slices in a colander and sprinkle generously with salt. Let them sit for about 30 minutes to draw out the bitterness. Rinse the eggplant slices under cold water and pat them dry with paper towels.
2. **Coat the eggplant**: Set up a breading station with three shallow bowls. Place the flour in the first bowl, beaten eggs in the second bowl, and breadcrumbs mixed with grated Parmesan cheese in the third bowl. Dredge each eggplant slice in the flour, then dip into the beaten eggs, and finally coat evenly with the breadcrumb mixture, pressing gently to adhere.
3. **Fry the eggplant**: In a large skillet, heat enough olive oil over medium heat to cover the bottom of the pan. Fry the breaded eggplant slices in batches until golden brown and crispy on both sides, about 3-4 minutes per side. Transfer to a paper towel-lined plate to drain excess oil.
4. **Assemble the Eggplant Parmesan**: Preheat your oven to 375°F (190°C). Spread a thin layer of marinara sauce on the bottom of a 9x13 inch baking dish. Arrange a layer of fried eggplant slices over the sauce. Top each slice with a spoonful of marinara sauce and a sprinkle of shredded mozzarella cheese. Repeat layers until all the eggplant slices are used, ending with a layer of marinara sauce and shredded mozzarella cheese on top.
5. **Bake**: Cover the baking dish with aluminum foil and bake in the preheated oven for 25 minutes. Remove the foil and bake for an additional 10-15 minutes, or until the cheese is melted and bubbly.
6. **Serve**: Let the Eggplant Parmesan cool slightly before serving. Garnish with chopped fresh basil leaves if desired. Serve hot as a main dish with a side of salad or crusty bread.

Tips:

- **Slicing**: Try to slice the eggplant evenly so that they cook uniformly.
- **Breading**: Ensure each slice of eggplant is well-coated with breadcrumbs for a crispy texture.
- **Variations**: You can add a layer of ricotta cheese or fresh mozzarella slices between the eggplant layers for added creaminess.

Eggplant Parmesan is a delicious and hearty dish that's perfect for a satisfying dinner. Enjoy this classic Italian favorite!

Cucumber Avocado Salad

Ingredients:

- 2 large cucumbers, sliced
- 2 ripe avocados, diced
- 1/4 cup red onion, thinly sliced
- 1/4 cup cherry tomatoes, halved
- 2 tablespoons fresh cilantro or parsley, chopped
- Juice of 1 lime (about 2 tablespoons)
- 2 tablespoons extra virgin olive oil
- Salt and pepper, to taste
- Optional: crumbled feta cheese or goat cheese for topping

Instructions:

1. **Prepare the vegetables**: Slice the cucumbers into thin rounds. Dice the avocados and thinly slice the red onion. Halve the cherry tomatoes. Chop the cilantro or parsley.
2. **Make the dressing**: In a small bowl, whisk together the lime juice, extra virgin olive oil, salt, and pepper until well combined.
3. **Assemble the salad**: In a large salad bowl, combine the sliced cucumbers, diced avocados, sliced red onion, cherry tomatoes, and chopped cilantro or parsley.
4. **Add dressing**: Pour the dressing over the salad ingredients. Gently toss the salad until everything is evenly coated with the dressing.
5. **Serve**: Serve the cucumber avocado salad immediately, optionally topped with crumbled feta cheese or goat cheese for added flavor.

Tips:

- **Avocado**: Choose ripe but firm avocados for best texture.
- **Variations**: You can add other vegetables like bell peppers, radishes, or arugula to the salad for more flavor and texture.
- **Storage**: If making ahead of time, wait to add the avocado until just before serving to prevent browning. Store any leftovers in an airtight container in the refrigerator for up to a day.

This cucumber avocado salad is perfect as a side dish or a light lunch, especially during warmer months when fresh and cool dishes are especially appealing. Enjoy!

Lentil Soup

Ingredients:

- 1 cup dried lentils (green or brown), rinsed and picked over
- 2 tablespoons olive oil
- 1 onion, chopped
- 2 carrots, diced
- 2 celery stalks, diced
- 3 cloves garlic, minced
- 1 teaspoon ground cumin
- 1 teaspoon ground coriander
- 1/2 teaspoon smoked paprika (optional, for added flavor)
- 6 cups vegetable broth or chicken broth
- 1 can (14 ounces) diced tomatoes
- Salt and pepper, to taste
- Fresh lemon juice, to taste (optional)
- Fresh parsley or cilantro, chopped (for garnish)

Instructions:

1. **Sauté vegetables**: In a large pot or Dutch oven, heat the olive oil over medium heat. Add the chopped onion, carrots, and celery. Sauté for about 5-7 minutes until the vegetables begin to soften.
2. **Add garlic and spices**: Add the minced garlic, ground cumin, ground coriander, and smoked paprika (if using). Stir constantly for about 1 minute until fragrant.
3. **Add lentils and broth**: Add the rinsed lentils, vegetable or chicken broth, and diced tomatoes (with their juices) to the pot. Stir to combine.
4. **Simmer**: Bring the soup to a boil, then reduce the heat to low. Cover and simmer for about 25-30 minutes, or until the lentils are tender.
5. **Season**: Taste the soup and season with salt and pepper to your liking. Add a squeeze of fresh lemon juice for brightness, if desired.
6. **Serve**: Ladle the lentil soup into bowls. Garnish with chopped fresh parsley or cilantro.

Tips:

- **Variations**: You can add diced potatoes, spinach, kale, or diced ham for additional flavor and texture.
- **Texture**: If you prefer a smoother soup, use an immersion blender to blend a portion of the soup until it reaches your desired consistency.
- **Storage**: Lentil soup stores well and can be kept in an airtight container in the refrigerator for up to 4-5 days. It also freezes well for longer storage.

This lentil soup recipe is versatile, nutritious, and perfect for a comforting meal. Enjoy it with crusty bread or a side salad for a complete and satisfying dish.

Chicken Quesadillas

Ingredients:

- 2 cups cooked chicken breast, shredded or diced
- 1 cup shredded cheese (cheddar, Monterey Jack, or a blend)
- 1/2 cup diced bell peppers (any color)
- 1/4 cup diced red onion
- 1 teaspoon ground cumin
- 1 teaspoon chili powder
- 1/2 teaspoon garlic powder
- Salt and pepper, to taste
- 4 large flour tortillas (10-inch size)
- 2 tablespoons vegetable oil (for cooking)

Optional toppings:

- Sour cream
- Salsa
- Guacamole
- Chopped cilantro
- Diced tomatoes

Instructions:

1. **Prepare the filling**: In a mixing bowl, combine the cooked chicken, shredded cheese, diced bell peppers, diced red onion, ground cumin, chili powder, garlic powder, salt, and pepper. Mix well to combine.
2. **Assemble the quesadillas**: Place a tortilla on a flat surface. Spread about 1/4 of the chicken and cheese mixture evenly over one half of the tortilla, leaving a small border around the edges. Fold the other half of the tortilla over the filling to create a half-moon shape.
3. **Cook the quesadillas**: Heat 1 tablespoon of vegetable oil in a large skillet over medium heat. Carefully place one quesadilla in the skillet and cook for about 2-3 minutes on each side, or until the tortilla is golden brown and the cheese is melted. Repeat with the remaining quesadillas, adding more oil to the skillet as needed.
4. **Serve**: Remove the quesadillas from the skillet and let them cool for a minute before slicing into wedges. Serve hot with optional toppings like sour cream, salsa, guacamole, chopped cilantro, or diced tomatoes.

Tips:

- **Variations**: You can customize your chicken quesadillas by adding ingredients like black beans, corn, jalapeños, or diced avocado.

- **Storage**: Quesadillas are best enjoyed fresh, but any leftovers can be stored in an airtight container in the refrigerator for a day or two. Reheat them in a skillet over medium heat until warmed through.

Chicken quesadillas are versatile and perfect for a quick meal or a casual get-together. They're easy to make and always a crowd-pleaser! Enjoy your homemade chicken quesadillas with your favorite toppings.

Pineapple Fried Rice

Ingredients:

- 2 cups cooked rice (preferably cold, such as jasmine or long-grain rice)
- 1 cup pineapple chunks (fresh or canned)
- 1 bell pepper (any color), diced
- 1 carrot, diced
- 1/2 cup frozen peas, thawed
- 2 cloves garlic, minced
- 2 green onions, chopped
- 1/4 cup cashews or peanuts, chopped (optional, for garnish)
- 2 eggs, lightly beaten
- 2 tablespoons soy sauce
- 1 tablespoon fish sauce (optional, for extra umami)
- 1 tablespoon curry powder
- Salt and pepper, to taste
- 2 tablespoons vegetable oil, divided

Instructions:

1. **Prepare the rice**: If you haven't already cooked the rice, cook it according to package instructions and let it cool completely. Cold rice works best for fried rice as it separates easily.
2. **Heat a large skillet or wok**: Heat 1 tablespoon of vegetable oil over medium-high heat. Add the beaten eggs and scramble them until they are cooked through. Remove the scrambled eggs from the skillet and set them aside.
3. **Sauté vegetables**: In the same skillet or wok, add the remaining tablespoon of vegetable oil. Add the minced garlic and sauté for about 30 seconds until fragrant. Add the diced bell pepper and carrot. Stir-fry for 3-4 minutes until they begin to soften.
4. **Add pineapple and peas**: Add the pineapple chunks and thawed peas to the skillet. Stir-fry for another 1-2 minutes until heated through.
5. **Add rice and seasonings**: Add the cooked rice to the skillet, breaking up any clumps with a spatula. Drizzle soy sauce and fish sauce (if using) over the rice. Sprinkle curry powder, salt, and pepper over the mixture. Stir-fry for 3-4 minutes until everything is well combined and heated through.
6. **Combine scrambled eggs and green onions**: Add the scrambled eggs back to the skillet. Stir in chopped green onions and toss everything together until evenly distributed.
7. **Serve**: Transfer the pineapple fried rice to serving plates or a large serving dish. Garnish with chopped cashews or peanuts if desired. Serve hot and enjoy!

Tips:

- **Variations**: You can add shrimp, chicken, or tofu for added protein. Cook the protein separately and add it to the fried rice at the end.
- **Pineapple**: Fresh pineapple adds a vibrant sweetness, but canned pineapple works well too.
- **Storage**: Leftover pineapple fried rice can be stored in an airtight container in the refrigerator for up to 3 days. Reheat gently in the microwave or in a skillet with a bit of oil.

Pineapple fried rice is a delicious and satisfying dish that's perfect for a quick weeknight meal or for entertaining guests. Enjoy the blend of flavors and textures in this delightful recipe!

Cabbage Stir-Fry

Ingredients:

- 1/2 head of cabbage, thinly sliced
- 1 carrot, julienned or thinly sliced
- 1 bell pepper (any color), thinly sliced
- 1 onion, thinly sliced
- 2 cloves garlic, minced
- 1-inch piece of ginger, grated or minced
- 2 tablespoons soy sauce
- 1 tablespoon oyster sauce (optional, for added flavor)
- 1 tablespoon sesame oil
- 2 tablespoons vegetable oil
- Salt and pepper, to taste
- Optional: red pepper flakes or Sriracha for heat, sesame seeds for garnish

Instructions:

1. **Prepare vegetables:** Thinly slice the cabbage, julienne or thinly slice the carrot, thinly slice the bell pepper, and thinly slice the onion. Mince the garlic and grate or mince the ginger.
2. **Heat vegetable oil:** Heat the vegetable oil in a large skillet or wok over medium-high heat.
3. **Sauté aromatics:** Add the minced garlic and grated ginger to the skillet. Stir-fry for about 30 seconds until fragrant.
4. **Add vegetables:** Add the sliced onion and bell pepper to the skillet. Stir-fry for 2-3 minutes until they begin to soften.
5. **Add cabbage:** Add the thinly sliced cabbage to the skillet. Stir-fry for another 3-4 minutes until the cabbage starts to wilt but still has some crunch.
6. **Add sauces:** Drizzle soy sauce and oyster sauce (if using) over the vegetables. Stir to combine and coat the vegetables evenly. Cook for another 1-2 minutes.
7. **Season:** Taste and season with salt and pepper as needed. If you like it spicy, add red pepper flakes or Sriracha to taste.
8. **Finish with sesame oil:** Drizzle sesame oil over the stir-fry and toss to combine. Remove from heat.
9. **Serve:** Transfer the cabbage stir-fry to a serving dish. Garnish with sesame seeds if desired. Serve hot as a side dish or over rice as a main course.

Tips:

- **Variations:** You can add other vegetables like mushrooms, snow peas, or bean sprouts for added texture and flavor.
- **Protein:** Add cooked chicken, shrimp, or tofu to make it a complete meal.

- **Storage:** Leftover cabbage stir-fry can be stored in an airtight container in the refrigerator for up to 3 days. Reheat gently in a skillet or microwave before serving.

This cabbage stir-fry recipe is versatile and can be customized based on your preferences. It's a nutritious and tasty way to enjoy cabbage as part of your meal!

Sausage and Peppers

Ingredients:

- 1 pound Italian sausage links (sweet or spicy), sliced into 1-inch pieces
- 2 bell peppers (any color), thinly sliced
- 1 large onion, thinly sliced
- 3 cloves garlic, minced
- 1 can (14.5 ounces) diced tomatoes
- 1/2 cup chicken broth or white wine
- 1 teaspoon dried oregano
- 1 teaspoon dried basil
- Salt and pepper, to taste
- 2 tablespoons olive oil
- Fresh parsley, chopped (for garnish)
- Cooked rice, pasta, or crusty bread (for serving)

Instructions:

1. **Sauté sausage:** Heat 1 tablespoon of olive oil in a large skillet or Dutch oven over medium-high heat. Add the sliced sausage pieces and cook until browned on all sides, about 5-7 minutes. Remove the sausage from the skillet and set aside.
2. **Sauté vegetables:** In the same skillet, add the remaining tablespoon of olive oil. Add the sliced bell peppers and onion. Sauté for about 5 minutes, until the vegetables begin to soften.
3. **Add garlic and seasonings:** Add the minced garlic, dried oregano, and dried basil to the skillet. Cook for another 1-2 minutes until the garlic is fragrant.
4. **Deglaze the skillet:** Pour in the chicken broth or white wine to deglaze the skillet, scraping up any browned bits from the bottom with a wooden spoon.
5. **Simmer:** Add the diced tomatoes (with their juices) to the skillet. Bring the mixture to a simmer and cook for about 10 minutes, allowing the flavors to meld and the sauce to thicken slightly.
6. **Add sausage back:** Return the cooked sausage pieces to the skillet. Stir to combine with the vegetables and sauce. Cook for an additional 5 minutes to heat through.
7. **Season and garnish:** Taste and season with salt and pepper as needed. Garnish with chopped fresh parsley.
8. **Serve:** Serve the sausage and peppers hot over cooked rice, pasta, or with crusty bread on the side.

Tips:

- **Variations:** You can add sliced mushrooms, zucchini, or diced tomatoes for additional flavor and texture.
- **Spice level:** Adjust the spiciness by choosing mild or spicy Italian sausage.

- **Storage:** Leftovers can be stored in an airtight container in the refrigerator for up to 3 days. Reheat gently on the stove or in the microwave before serving.

Sausage and peppers is a comforting and satisfying dish that's perfect for a family dinner or casual gathering. Enjoy the delicious combination of flavors!

Mango Salsa

Ingredients:

- 2 ripe mangoes, peeled, pitted, and diced
- 1/2 red bell pepper, diced
- 1/2 red onion, finely chopped
- 1 jalapeño pepper, seeded and finely chopped (adjust amount based on spice preference)
- 1/4 cup fresh cilantro, chopped
- Juice of 1 lime
- Salt and pepper, to taste

Instructions:

1. **Prepare the mango and vegetables:**
    - Peel, pit, and dice the mangoes. Dice the red bell pepper and finely chop the red onion and jalapeño pepper. Chop the fresh cilantro.
2. **Combine ingredients:**
    - In a medium bowl, combine the diced mangoes, diced red bell pepper, finely chopped red onion, finely chopped jalapeño pepper, and chopped cilantro.
3. **Add lime juice and seasonings:**
    - Squeeze the juice of one lime over the salsa mixture. Season with salt and pepper to taste.
4. **Mix well:**
    - Gently toss all the ingredients together until well combined.
5. **Chill (optional):**
    - For best flavor, you can refrigerate the mango salsa for about 30 minutes to allow the flavors to meld together.
6. **Serve:**
    - Serve the mango salsa immediately as a topping for grilled chicken, fish, or tacos. Alternatively, enjoy it as a dip with tortilla chips.

Tips:

- **Adjust heat:** The spiciness of the salsa can be adjusted by adding more or less jalapeño pepper. For a milder salsa, remove the seeds and membranes from the jalapeño before chopping.
- **Variations:** You can add diced avocado, cucumber, or black beans for additional texture and flavor.
- **Storage:** Store leftover mango salsa in an airtight container in the refrigerator. It's best enjoyed fresh but can typically be kept for up to 2 days.

Mango salsa is vibrant, tangy, and adds a burst of tropical flavor to any dish. It's perfect for summer gatherings or anytime you want to add a refreshing twist to your meals. Enjoy this delicious mango salsa recipe!

Spinach and Feta Stuffed Chicken

Ingredients:

- 4 boneless, skinless chicken breasts
- Salt and pepper, to taste
- 2 cups fresh spinach leaves, chopped
- 1/2 cup crumbled feta cheese
- 1/4 cup grated Parmesan cheese
- 2 cloves garlic, minced
- 1 tablespoon olive oil
- 1 tablespoon butter
- 1/4 teaspoon dried oregano
- 1/4 teaspoon dried basil
- Toothpicks or kitchen twine (optional, for securing chicken)

Instructions:

1. **Preheat oven:** Preheat your oven to 375°F (190°C).
2. **Prepare chicken breasts:** Using a sharp knife, make a horizontal slit along the side of each chicken breast to create a pocket for the stuffing. Be careful not to cut all the way through.
3. **Season chicken:** Season the inside and outside of each chicken breast with salt and pepper.
4. **Make the spinach and feta filling:**
    - In a skillet, heat olive oil over medium heat. Add minced garlic and sauté for about 30 seconds until fragrant.
    - Add chopped spinach to the skillet and cook until wilted, about 2-3 minutes.
    - Remove from heat and stir in crumbled feta cheese, grated Parmesan cheese, dried oregano, and dried basil. Mix until well combined.
5. **Stuff the chicken breasts:**
    - Divide the spinach and feta filling evenly among the chicken breasts, spooning it into the pockets you created earlier. Secure the openings with toothpicks or kitchen twine if necessary to hold the filling inside.
6. **Sear the chicken:**
    - In the same skillet, melt butter over medium-high heat. Add the stuffed chicken breasts and sear on each side for about 2-3 minutes until golden brown.
7. **Bake:**
    - Transfer the seared chicken breasts to a baking dish. Bake in the preheated oven for 20-25 minutes, or until the chicken is cooked through (internal temperature of 165°F or 74°C).
8. **Serve:**

- Remove the toothpicks or twine before serving. Optionally, garnish with fresh herbs like parsley or basil. Serve the spinach and feta stuffed chicken hot, alongside your favorite side dishes.

Tips:

- **Variations:** You can add sun-dried tomatoes, chopped olives, or pine nuts to the spinach and feta filling for extra flavor and texture.
- **Side dishes:** Serve with roasted vegetables, rice, or a side salad for a complete meal.
- **Storage:** Store any leftovers in an airtight container in the refrigerator for up to 3 days. Reheat gently in the oven or microwave before serving.

Spinach and feta stuffed chicken is a wonderful dish for a special dinner or when you want to impress guests with a flavorful and wholesome meal. Enjoy!

Ratatouille

Ingredients:

- 1 large eggplant, diced
- 2 zucchinis, diced
- 1 red bell pepper, diced
- 1 yellow bell pepper, diced
- 1 onion, diced
- 4 cloves garlic, minced
- 4 tomatoes, diced (or 1 can (14 oz) diced tomatoes)
- 2 tablespoons tomato paste
- 1 teaspoon dried thyme
- 1 teaspoon dried oregano
- 1 bay leaf
- Salt and pepper, to taste
- 2 tablespoons olive oil
- Fresh basil, chopped (for garnish)

Instructions:

1. **Prepare the vegetables:**
   - Dice the eggplant, zucchinis, red bell pepper, yellow bell pepper, and onion into similar-sized pieces.
2. **Sauté the onions and garlic:**
   - Heat 1 tablespoon of olive oil in a large pot or Dutch oven over medium heat. Add the diced onion and cook for 3-4 minutes until softened. Add the minced garlic and cook for another 1-2 minutes until fragrant.
3. **Cook the vegetables:**
   - Push the onions and garlic to the side of the pot and add the remaining tablespoon of olive oil. Add the diced eggplant, zucchinis, red bell pepper, and yellow bell pepper. Cook, stirring occasionally, for about 8-10 minutes until the vegetables start to soften.
4. **Add tomatoes and seasonings:**
   - Add the diced tomatoes (or canned tomatoes) to the pot, along with tomato paste, dried thyme, dried oregano, bay leaf, salt, and pepper. Stir well to combine.
5. **Simmer:**
   - Bring the mixture to a simmer, then reduce the heat to low. Cover the pot and let the ratatouille simmer gently for 30-40 minutes, stirring occasionally, until the vegetables are tender and the flavors have melded together.
6. **Adjust seasoning:**
   - Taste and adjust seasoning with salt and pepper if needed.
7. **Serve:**

- Remove the bay leaf before serving. Garnish with freshly chopped basil.

Tips:

- **Variations:** Ratatouille can be served hot, warm, or even chilled. It can be enjoyed on its own, as a side dish, or with crusty bread or rice.
- **Storage:** Leftover ratatouille can be stored in an airtight container in the refrigerator for up to 3-4 days. It also freezes well for longer storage.
- **Enhancements:** Some recipes include additional herbs like rosemary or parsley. You can also add a drizzle of balsamic vinegar or sprinkle with grated Parmesan cheese before serving for extra flavor.

Ratatouille is a versatile and comforting dish that celebrates the flavors of fresh vegetables. It's a wonderful way to enjoy seasonal produce and makes a satisfying meal any time of year.

Cilantro Lime Rice

Ingredients:

- 1 cup long-grain white rice (such as jasmine or basmati)
- 1 3/4 cups water or chicken broth
- 1 tablespoon butter or olive oil
- 1/2 teaspoon salt, or to taste
- Zest and juice of 1 lime
- 1/4 cup fresh cilantro, finely chopped

Instructions:

1. **Rinse the rice:** Rinse the rice under cold water until the water runs clear. This helps remove excess starch for fluffier rice.
2. **Cook the rice:** In a medium saucepan, combine the rinsed rice, water or chicken broth, butter or olive oil, and salt. Bring to a boil over medium-high heat.
3. **Simmer:** Once boiling, reduce the heat to low, cover, and simmer for 15-20 minutes, or until the rice is tender and the liquid is absorbed.
4. **Fluff the rice:** Remove the saucepan from heat and let it sit, covered, for 5 minutes. Then, uncover and fluff the rice with a fork.
5. **Add lime and cilantro:** Add the lime zest, lime juice, and finely chopped cilantro to the rice. Gently toss with a fork to combine evenly.
6. **Adjust seasoning:** Taste the rice and adjust seasoning with additional salt or lime juice if desired.
7. **Serve:** Transfer the cilantro lime rice to a serving bowl and garnish with additional chopped cilantro if desired. Serve hot as a side dish with your favorite Mexican or Tex-Mex dishes.

Tips:

- **Variations:** For extra flavor, you can add a minced clove of garlic or a diced jalapeño to the rice while cooking.
- **Storage:** Leftover cilantro lime rice can be stored in an airtight container in the refrigerator for up to 3-4 days. Reheat gently in the microwave or on the stovetop with a splash of water.
- **Serve with:** Cilantro lime rice pairs well with dishes like grilled chicken, fish tacos, burritos, or as a base for a rice bowl with beans and vegetables.

Cilantro lime rice is fresh, vibrant, and adds a burst of flavor to any meal. It's easy to make at home and a versatile addition to your recipe repertoire!

Chickpea Curry

Ingredients:

- 2 tablespoons vegetable oil
- 1 large onion, finely chopped
- 3 cloves garlic, minced
- 1-inch piece of ginger, grated or minced
- 2 teaspoons ground cumin
- 1 teaspoon ground coriander
- 1/2 teaspoon turmeric powder
- 1/2 teaspoon paprika (or cayenne pepper for spicier curry)
- 1/2 teaspoon garam masala
- 1/4 teaspoon ground cinnamon
- 1/4 teaspoon ground cloves
- 1/4 teaspoon ground cardamom
- 1 can (15 ounces) chickpeas, drained and rinsed (or about 1.5 cups cooked chickpeas)
- 1 can (14 ounces) diced tomatoes
- 1/2 cup coconut milk (optional, for creamier curry)
- Salt, to taste
- Fresh cilantro, chopped (for garnish)

Instructions:

1. **Sauté onions, garlic, and ginger:**
    - Heat vegetable oil in a large skillet or pot over medium heat. Add the finely chopped onion and sauté for 5-6 minutes until softened and translucent.
    - Add minced garlic and grated ginger. Sauté for another 1-2 minutes until fragrant.
2. **Add spices:**
    - Add ground cumin, ground coriander, turmeric powder, paprika (or cayenne pepper), garam masala, ground cinnamon, ground cloves, and ground cardamom to the skillet. Stir well to coat the onions and cook the spices for 1 minute until fragrant.
3. **Cook chickpeas:**
    - Add the drained and rinsed chickpeas to the skillet. Stir to combine with the onion and spice mixture.
4. **Add tomatoes:**
    - Pour in the diced tomatoes with their juices. Stir well and bring the mixture to a simmer. Reduce heat to low and let it simmer uncovered for 10-15 minutes, stirring occasionally, until the sauce thickens slightly.
5. **Add coconut milk (optional):**
    - If using coconut milk for a creamier curry, pour it into the skillet and stir to combine. Let it simmer for another 5 minutes. Adjust the consistency with water if needed.

6. **Season with salt:**
   - Taste the chickpea curry and season with salt according to your preference.
7. **Finish and serve:**
   - Remove the skillet from heat. Garnish with chopped fresh cilantro before serving.
8. **Serve:**
   - Serve the chickpea curry hot with steamed rice or naan bread. Enjoy the flavors and aroma of this comforting dish!

Tips:

- **Variations:** You can add spinach, diced potatoes, or bell peppers to the curry for added texture and nutrition.
- **Spice level:** Adjust the amount of paprika or cayenne pepper to your preferred spice level.
- **Storage:** Leftover chickpea curry can be stored in an airtight container in the refrigerator for up to 3-4 days. Reheat gently on the stove or in the microwave before serving.

Chickpea curry is a wholesome and satisfying dish that's rich in flavors and perfect for vegetarians and vegans alike. Enjoy this hearty meal as a main course or part of a larger Indian-inspired feast!

Bruschetta

Ingredients:

- 4-5 ripe tomatoes, diced
- 1-2 cloves garlic, minced
- 6-8 fresh basil leaves, chopped
- 2 tablespoons extra virgin olive oil
- 1 teaspoon balsamic vinegar (optional)
- Salt and pepper, to taste
- 1 baguette or Italian bread, sliced
- Olive oil, for brushing

Instructions:

1. **Prepare the tomato topping:**
   - In a mixing bowl, combine the diced tomatoes, minced garlic, chopped basil leaves, extra virgin olive oil, and balsamic vinegar (if using).
   - Season with salt and pepper to taste. Stir well to combine all the ingredients. Set aside to let the flavors meld together while you prepare the bread.
2. **Toast the bread:**
   - Preheat your oven to 400°F (200°C). Arrange the bread slices on a baking sheet in a single layer.
   - Brush both sides of each bread slice lightly with olive oil.
3. **Bake the bread:**
   - Place the baking sheet in the preheated oven and bake for 5-7 minutes, or until the bread slices are golden and crisp. Flip the slices halfway through baking for even toasting.
4. **Assemble the bruschetta:**
   - Once the bread slices are toasted, remove them from the oven and let them cool slightly.
   - Spoon the tomato mixture generously over each toasted bread slice. Ensure each slice gets a good amount of tomatoes, garlic, and basil.
5. **Serve:**
   - Arrange the bruschetta on a serving platter. Optionally, garnish with additional fresh basil leaves or a drizzle of balsamic glaze.
   - Serve immediately as an appetizer or snack.

Tips:

- **Variations:** You can customize your bruschetta by adding ingredients like mozzarella cheese, olives, capers, or red onion.
- **Make ahead:** You can prepare the tomato topping ahead of time and store it in the refrigerator. Toast the bread slices just before serving to keep them crisp.

- **Storage:** Store leftover tomato topping in an airtight container in the refrigerator for up to 2 days. Toasted bread should be stored in a sealed container at room temperature.

Bruschetta is a wonderful dish that highlights the freshness of tomatoes and herbs. It's perfect for entertaining guests or enjoying as a light and flavorful appetizer. Enjoy your homemade bruschetta!

Zucchini Noodles with Marinara

Ingredients:

- 4 medium zucchini
- 2 tablespoons olive oil
- 2 cloves garlic, minced
- 1/2 teaspoon red pepper flakes (optional, for heat)
- 2 cups marinara sauce (homemade or store-bought)
- Salt and pepper, to taste
- Grated Parmesan cheese, for serving
- Fresh basil leaves, chopped, for garnish

Instructions:

1. **Prepare the zucchini noodles:**
    - Using a spiralizer, julienne peeler, or vegetable peeler, make zucchini noodles (zoodles) from the zucchini. If using a spiralizer, follow the manufacturer's instructions. If using a julienne peeler or vegetable peeler, carefully peel the zucchini lengthwise into long, thin strips.
2. **Cook the zucchini noodles:**
    - Heat 1 tablespoon of olive oil in a large skillet over medium heat. Add the minced garlic and red pepper flakes (if using). Sauté for about 1 minute until the garlic is fragrant.
    - Add the zucchini noodles to the skillet. Sauté for 2-3 minutes, tossing gently with tongs, until the zoodles are just tender but still crisp. Season with salt and pepper to taste. Be careful not to overcook, as zucchini noodles can become mushy.
3. **Heat the marinara sauce:**
    - In a separate saucepan, heat the marinara sauce over medium heat until warmed through.
4. **Combine zucchini noodles and marinara sauce:**
    - Pour the warmed marinara sauce over the cooked zucchini noodles in the skillet. Toss gently to coat the zoodles evenly with the sauce.
5. **Serve:**
    - Divide the zucchini noodles with marinara sauce among serving plates.
    - Garnish with grated Parmesan cheese and chopped fresh basil leaves.
6. **Enjoy:**
    - Serve immediately as a light and healthy meal. Enjoy the flavors of the zucchini noodles with the savory marinara sauce!

Tips:

- **Variations:** You can add cooked chicken, shrimp, or tofu for added protein. Sauté them separately and add them to the zucchini noodles and marinara sauce at the end.

- **Extra flavor:** Enhance the marinara sauce with additional herbs like oregano, basil, or thyme.
- **Storage:** Store any leftover zucchini noodles and marinara sauce separately in airtight containers in the refrigerator. Reheat gently in a skillet or microwave before serving.

Zucchini noodles with marinara sauce is a nutritious and satisfying dish that's perfect for a light lunch or dinner. It's low-carb, gluten-free, and packed with fresh flavors. Enjoy this healthy alternative to pasta!

Stuffed Mushrooms

Ingredients:

- 12 large mushrooms (cremini or button mushrooms)
- 1 tablespoon olive oil
- 2 cloves garlic, minced
- 1/4 cup finely chopped onion
- 1/4 cup finely chopped red bell pepper
- 1/4 cup finely chopped celery
- 1/4 cup breadcrumbs (plain or seasoned)
- 1/4 cup grated Parmesan cheese
- 2 tablespoons chopped fresh parsley
- Salt and pepper, to taste
- 2 tablespoons butter, melted

Instructions:

1. **Prepare the mushrooms:**
    - Preheat your oven to 375°F (190°C). Line a baking sheet with parchment paper or aluminum foil.
    - Clean the mushrooms with a damp cloth to remove any dirt. Remove the stems from the mushrooms and finely chop them. Set aside.
2. **Prepare the filling:**
    - In a skillet, heat olive oil over medium heat. Add minced garlic, chopped onion, red bell pepper, and celery. Sauté for about 5 minutes until the vegetables are softened.
3. **Make the stuffing mixture:**
    - Add the chopped mushroom stems to the skillet and cook for another 3-4 minutes, until they release their moisture and the mixture is fragrant.
    - Remove the skillet from heat and stir in breadcrumbs, grated Parmesan cheese, chopped parsley, salt, and pepper. Mix well to combine.
4. **Stuff the mushrooms:**
    - Using a spoon, fill each mushroom cap generously with the stuffing mixture, pressing gently to pack it in.
5. **Bake the stuffed mushrooms:**
    - Place the stuffed mushrooms on the prepared baking sheet. Drizzle melted butter over the stuffed mushrooms.
6. **Bake in the oven:**
    - Bake the stuffed mushrooms in the preheated oven for 20-25 minutes, or until the mushrooms are tender and the tops are golden brown.
7. **Serve:**
    - Remove the stuffed mushrooms from the oven and let them cool slightly before serving.

- Garnish with additional chopped parsley if desired.
- Serve warm as an appetizer or side dish.

Tips:

- **Variations:** You can customize the stuffing by adding ingredients like cooked sausage, chopped spinach, sun-dried tomatoes, or different types of cheese.
- **Make ahead:** Prepare the stuffing mixture ahead of time and store it in the refrigerator. Stuff the mushrooms and bake them just before serving.
- **Storage:** Leftover stuffed mushrooms can be stored in an airtight container in the refrigerator for up to 2 days. Reheat gently in the oven or microwave before serving.

Stuffed mushrooms are a crowd-pleasing dish that's perfect for parties, gatherings, or simply as a delicious appetizer. Enjoy the savory flavors and tender texture of these stuffed mushrooms!

Corn and Black Bean Salad

Ingredients:

- 1 can (15 ounces) black beans, rinsed and drained
- 1 cup corn kernels (fresh, canned, or frozen)
- 1 red bell pepper, diced
- 1/2 red onion, finely chopped
- 1 jalapeño pepper, seeded and finely chopped (optional, for heat)
- 1/4 cup fresh cilantro, chopped
- Juice of 1 lime (about 2 tablespoons)
- 2 tablespoons olive oil
- 1 teaspoon ground cumin
- 1/2 teaspoon chili powder
- Salt and pepper, to taste
- Avocado slices, for garnish (optional)

Instructions:

1. **Prepare the salad:**
   - In a large mixing bowl, combine the black beans, corn kernels, diced red bell pepper, finely chopped red onion, chopped jalapeño pepper (if using), and chopped fresh cilantro.
2. **Make the dressing:**
   - In a small bowl, whisk together the lime juice, olive oil, ground cumin, chili powder, salt, and pepper until well combined.
3. **Combine salad and dressing:**
   - Pour the dressing over the salad ingredients in the large mixing bowl. Toss gently to coat everything evenly with the dressing.
4. **Chill (optional):**
   - For best flavor, cover the bowl with plastic wrap or transfer the salad to a sealed container and refrigerate for at least 30 minutes to allow the flavors to meld together.
5. **Serve:**
   - Before serving, taste and adjust seasoning with additional salt, pepper, or lime juice if needed.
   - Garnish with avocado slices if desired.
6. **Enjoy:**
   - Serve the corn and black bean salad chilled or at room temperature as a side dish, appetizer with tortilla chips, or as a topping for tacos or grilled meats.

Tips:

- **Variations:** You can add diced tomatoes, chopped green onions, or a dash of hot sauce for additional flavor and color.
- **Make ahead:** This salad can be made ahead of time and stored in the refrigerator for up to 2 days. Stir well before serving.
- **Protein boost:** For added protein, toss in cooked and shredded chicken or grilled shrimp.

Corn and black bean salad is vibrant, nutritious, and packed with fresh flavors. It's a versatile dish that's sure to be a hit at any gathering or meal. Enjoy this delicious and colorful salad!

Lemon Garlic Shrimp

Ingredients:

- 1 pound large shrimp, peeled and deveined
- 4 cloves garlic, minced
- Zest of 1 lemon
- Juice of 1 lemon
- 2 tablespoons olive oil
- 2 tablespoons butter
- Salt and pepper, to taste
- Fresh parsley, chopped, for garnish
- Lemon slices, for garnish (optional)

Instructions:

1. **Prepare the shrimp:**
   - Pat the shrimp dry with paper towels. Season with salt and pepper to taste.
2. **Heat the skillet:**
   - Heat olive oil in a large skillet over medium-high heat.
3. **Sauté the garlic:**
   - Add minced garlic to the skillet and sauté for about 1 minute until fragrant. Be careful not to burn the garlic.
4. **Cook the shrimp:**
   - Add the shrimp to the skillet in a single layer. Cook for 2-3 minutes, stirring occasionally, until the shrimp start to turn pink and opaque.
5. **Add lemon zest and juice:**
   - Stir in lemon zest and lemon juice. Cook for another 1-2 minutes until the shrimp are fully cooked and opaque.
6. **Finish with butter:**
   - Add butter to the skillet and stir until melted and well combined with the lemon garlic sauce.
7. **Garnish and serve:**
   - Remove the skillet from heat. Garnish with chopped fresh parsley and lemon slices (if using).
8. **Serve:**
   - Serve the lemon garlic shrimp immediately, either on its own or over pasta, rice, or with crusty bread to soak up the delicious sauce.

Tips:

- **Variations:** You can add red pepper flakes for a spicy kick, or chopped tomatoes for extra freshness.

- **Side dishes:** Lemon garlic shrimp pairs well with steamed vegetables, salad, or a side of garlic bread.
- **Storage:** Leftover lemon garlic shrimp can be stored in an airtight container in the refrigerator for up to 2 days. Reheat gently on the stove or in the microwave before serving.

Lemon garlic shrimp is a versatile dish that comes together quickly and is bursting with bright flavors. Enjoy this savory and satisfying meal any day of the week!

Potato Leek Soup

Ingredients:

- 3 leeks, white and light green parts only, cleaned and thinly sliced
- 3 tablespoons butter or olive oil
- 3-4 medium potatoes, peeled and diced
- 4 cups vegetable or chicken broth
- 1 cup milk or heavy cream (adjust amount based on desired creaminess)
- Salt and pepper, to taste
- Chopped chives or parsley, for garnish (optional)

Instructions:

1. **Prepare the leeks:**
   - Slice the leeks in half lengthwise and rinse them under cold water to remove any dirt or grit. Thinly slice the leeks.
2. **Sauté the leeks:**
   - In a large pot or Dutch oven, melt the butter (or heat olive oil) over medium heat. Add the sliced leeks and cook, stirring occasionally, for about 5-7 minutes until they are softened and translucent.
3. **Add potatoes and broth:**
   - Add the diced potatoes to the pot with the sautéed leeks. Pour in the vegetable or chicken broth, enough to cover the potatoes and leeks. Bring the mixture to a boil.
4. **Simmer:**
   - Reduce the heat to medium-low and simmer, uncovered, for about 15-20 minutes or until the potatoes are tender when pierced with a fork.
5. **Blend the soup (optional):**
   - At this point, you can choose to blend the soup until smooth using an immersion blender directly in the pot, or transfer the soup in batches to a blender. Blend until desired consistency is reached.
6. **Add milk or cream:**
   - Stir in the milk or heavy cream to the soup. Adjust the amount based on how creamy you want the soup to be. Heat through gently, but do not boil once the dairy is added.
7. **Season and serve:**
   - Season the soup with salt and pepper to taste. If desired, garnish with chopped chives or parsley before serving.
8. **Serve:**
   - Ladle the potato leek soup into bowls and serve hot. It pairs well with crusty bread or a side salad.

Tips:

- **Variations:** For extra flavor, you can add a dash of nutmeg or a sprinkle of thyme while cooking the soup.
- **Texture:** If you prefer a chunkier soup, you can mash some of the potatoes with a fork instead of blending the entire soup.
- **Storage:** Potato leek soup can be stored in the refrigerator for up to 3-4 days in an airtight container. Reheat gently on the stove, adding a splash of broth or milk to thin out if needed.

Potato leek soup is a comforting and versatile dish that's easy to make and full of rich, creamy flavors. Enjoy this soup as a satisfying meal any time of year!

BBQ Chicken Drumsticks

Ingredients:

- 8 chicken drumsticks
- 1 cup BBQ sauce (homemade or store-bought)
- 2 tablespoons olive oil
- 2 cloves garlic, minced
- 1 teaspoon paprika
- 1/2 teaspoon onion powder
- Salt and pepper, to taste
- Fresh parsley or cilantro, chopped for garnish (optional)

Instructions:

1. **Prepare the chicken drumsticks:**
   - Pat the chicken drumsticks dry with paper towels. Season them generously with salt and pepper.
2. **Marinate the chicken:**
   - In a bowl, combine olive oil, minced garlic, paprika, and onion powder. Mix well to create a marinade. Rub the marinade all over the chicken drumsticks, coating them evenly. Let them marinate for at least 30 minutes, or up to overnight in the refrigerator for more flavor.
3. **Preheat the grill:**
   - Preheat your grill to medium-high heat (about 375-400°F or 190-200°C).
4. **Grill the chicken:**
   - Place the marinated chicken drumsticks on the preheated grill. Close the lid and cook for about 20-25 minutes, turning occasionally, until the chicken is fully cooked through and reaches an internal temperature of 165°F (74°C).
5. **Apply BBQ sauce:**
   - During the last 5-10 minutes of grilling, brush the BBQ sauce generously onto the chicken drumsticks. Flip them and brush the other side with more BBQ sauce. Continue cooking until the sauce caramelizes slightly and forms a sticky glaze.
6. **Check for doneness:**

- To ensure the chicken is fully cooked, insert an instant-read thermometer into the thickest part of the drumstick. It should read 165°F (74°C).

7. **Serve:**
    - Remove the BBQ chicken drumsticks from the grill and transfer them to a serving platter. Sprinkle with chopped parsley or cilantro for garnish, if desired.
8. **Enjoy:**
    - Serve the BBQ chicken drumsticks hot, alongside your favorite sides like coleslaw, potato salad, or corn on the cob.

Tips:

- **Charcoal grill:** If using a charcoal grill, arrange the coals for direct heat and follow the same grilling instructions.
- **Oven alternative:** If you don't have a grill, you can bake the chicken drumsticks in the oven at 400°F (200°C) for 30-35 minutes, flipping halfway through and applying BBQ sauce in the last 10 minutes.
- **Storage:** Leftover BBQ chicken drumsticks can be stored in an airtight container in the refrigerator for up to 3-4 days. Reheat gently in the oven or microwave before serving.

BBQ chicken drumsticks are a crowd-pleasing dish that's easy to prepare and packed with smoky, sweet, and tangy flavors. Enjoy this classic BBQ favorite at your next gathering or weeknight meal!

Cauliflower Rice Stir-Fry

Ingredients:

- 1 medium head of cauliflower, or pre-riced cauliflower (about 4 cups of cauliflower rice)
- 1 tablespoon vegetable oil or olive oil
- 2 cloves garlic, minced
- 1 small onion, finely chopped
- 1 carrot, diced
- 1 bell pepper (any color), diced
- 1 cup frozen peas, thawed
- 2 eggs, lightly beaten (optional)
- 2-3 tablespoons soy sauce (adjust to taste)
- 1 teaspoon sesame oil (optional)
- Salt and pepper, to taste
- Green onions, chopped, for garnish (optional)
- Sesame seeds, for garnish (optional)

Instructions:

1. **Prepare the cauliflower rice:**

- If starting with a head of cauliflower, cut it into florets. Working in batches, pulse the cauliflower florets in a food processor until they resemble rice grains. Alternatively, you can use pre-riced cauliflower.
2. **Stir-fry the vegetables:**
    - Heat vegetable oil in a large skillet or wok over medium-high heat. Add minced garlic and chopped onion. Sauté for 2-3 minutes until fragrant and onion is translucent.
3. **Add remaining vegetables:**
    - Add diced carrot and bell pepper to the skillet. Stir-fry for another 3-4 minutes until they start to soften.
4. **Cook cauliflower rice:**
    - Add cauliflower rice and thawed peas to the skillet. Stir-fry for about 5-6 minutes, stirring frequently, until the cauliflower rice is tender but still has a slight crunch.
5. **Optional: Add eggs (if using):**
    - Push the cauliflower rice mixture to one side of the skillet. Pour beaten eggs into the empty side of the skillet. Allow them to set slightly, then scramble them until cooked through.
6. **Season with soy sauce and sesame oil:**
    - Drizzle soy sauce over the cauliflower rice mixture. Add sesame oil if using. Stir well to combine and coat everything evenly. Taste and adjust seasoning with salt and pepper if needed.
7. **Garnish and serve:**
    - Remove from heat. Garnish with chopped green onions and sesame seeds if desired.
8. **Serve hot:**
    - Serve cauliflower rice stir-fry immediately as a main dish or as a side dish with your favorite protein such as chicken, shrimp, or tofu.

Tips:

- **Variations:** You can customize your cauliflower rice stir-fry by adding other vegetables like broccoli, mushrooms, or snap peas.
- **Protein:** For added protein, toss in cooked chicken, shrimp, or tofu cubes during step 4.
- **Storage:** Leftover cauliflower rice stir-fry can be stored in an airtight container in the refrigerator for up to 3 days. Reheat gently in a skillet or microwave before serving.

Cauliflower rice stir-fry is a nutritious and satisfying dish that's quick and easy to make. Enjoy the crunchy texture and flavorful blend of vegetables in this low-carb alternative to rice stir-fry!

Italian Sausage Pasta

Ingredients:

- 12 ounces (340g) Italian sausage (sweet or spicy), casings removed
- 8 ounces (225g) pasta (such as penne, fusilli, or spaghetti)
- 1 tablespoon olive oil
- 1 small onion, finely chopped
- 2 cloves garlic, minced
- 1 can (14 ounces) diced tomatoes
- 1/2 cup tomato sauce
- 1 teaspoon dried oregano
- 1 teaspoon dried basil
- Salt and pepper, to taste
- 1/4 teaspoon red pepper flakes (optional, for heat)
- Grated Parmesan cheese, for serving
- Fresh basil or parsley, chopped, for garnish (optional)

Instructions:

1. **Cook the pasta:**
   - Cook the pasta according to package instructions in a large pot of salted boiling water until al dente. Drain and set aside, reserving 1/2 cup of pasta cooking water.
2. **Brown the sausage:**
   - In a large skillet or frying pan, heat olive oil over medium-high heat. Add the Italian sausage (casings removed) and cook, breaking it up with a spoon or spatula, until browned and cooked through, about 5-7 minutes. Transfer the cooked sausage to a plate lined with paper towels to drain excess grease.
3. **Sauté onion and garlic:**
   - In the same skillet, add chopped onion and minced garlic. Sauté for 2-3 minutes until softened and fragrant.
4. **Add tomatoes and sauce:**
   - Stir in diced tomatoes, tomato sauce, dried oregano, dried basil, salt, pepper, and red pepper flakes (if using). Bring the mixture to a simmer.
5. **Combine pasta and sausage:**
   - Add the cooked sausage back to the skillet with the tomato sauce. Stir to combine and let it simmer for another 5-7 minutes to allow the flavors to meld together. If the sauce seems too thick, add some of the reserved pasta cooking water to loosen it up.
6. **Finish and serve:**
   - Add the cooked pasta to the skillet with the sausage and sauce. Toss everything together until the pasta is well coated with the sauce.
7. **Garnish and serve:**

- Serve the Italian sausage pasta hot, garnished with grated Parmesan cheese and chopped fresh basil or parsley if desired.

Tips:

- **Variations:** You can add diced bell peppers, mushrooms, or spinach to the sauce for extra flavor and nutrients.
- **Spice level:** Adjust the amount of red pepper flakes according to your preference for heat.
- **Storage:** Leftover Italian sausage pasta can be stored in an airtight container in the refrigerator for up to 3 days. Reheat gently in a saucepan over low heat, adding a splash of water or broth to loosen the sauce.

Italian sausage pasta is a comforting and satisfying meal that's perfect for family dinners or entertaining guests. Enjoy the robust flavors of this classic Italian-inspired dish!

Hummus and Veggie Wraps

Ingredients:

- 4 large tortilla wraps (whole wheat or your preferred type)
- 1 cup hummus (store-bought or homemade)
- 1 cucumber, thinly sliced
- 1 bell pepper (any color), thinly sliced
- 1 large carrot, grated or thinly sliced
- 1/2 red onion, thinly sliced
- 1 cup mixed greens or lettuce
- Salt and pepper, to taste
- Optional: Sprouts, avocado slices, olives, or feta cheese

Instructions:

1. **Prepare the tortilla wraps:**
   - Lay out the tortilla wraps on a clean work surface.
2. **Spread hummus:**
   - Spread about 1/4 cup of hummus evenly over each tortilla wrap, leaving a small border around the edges.
3. **Layer the veggies:**
   - Divide the sliced cucumber, bell pepper, carrot, red onion, and mixed greens evenly among the wraps. Arrange the veggies in a single layer over the hummus.
4. **Season and add optional ingredients:**
   - Season the veggies with salt and pepper to taste. If desired, add additional ingredients like sprouts, avocado slices, olives, or crumbled feta cheese.
5. **Wrap the tortillas:**
   - Fold the sides of each tortilla towards the center, then roll up tightly from the bottom to form a wrap. Press gently to seal.
6. **Serve or store:**
   - Serve the hummus and veggie wraps immediately, or wrap them tightly in parchment paper or plastic wrap to store in the refrigerator for later. They can be stored for up to 1 day before serving.

Tips:

- **Variations:** You can customize your wraps with other veggies like spinach, tomatoes, shredded cabbage, or roasted vegetables.
- **Protein boost:** Add grilled chicken, tofu, chickpeas, or sliced hard-boiled eggs for added protein.
- **Dipping sauce:** Serve with extra hummus, tzatziki sauce, or a yogurt-based dressing on the side for dipping.

Hummus and veggie wraps are versatile, satisfying, and packed with crunchy fresh flavors. They make a great option for a healthy and portable meal that's easy to prepare and enjoy on the go!

Teriyaki Tofu

Ingredients:

- 1 block (14-16 ounces) firm or extra firm tofu
- 2 tablespoons soy sauce
- 2 tablespoons mirin (Japanese sweet rice wine) or rice vinegar
- 2 tablespoons honey or maple syrup
- 1 tablespoon sesame oil
- 2 cloves garlic, minced
- 1 teaspoon grated ginger
- 2 tablespoons water
- 1 tablespoon cornstarch (or arrowroot powder)
- 2 tablespoons vegetable oil, for frying
- Optional garnish: Sesame seeds, sliced green onions

Instructions:

1. **Prepare the tofu:**
    - Remove the tofu from the package and drain any excess water. Wrap the tofu block in paper towels or a clean kitchen towel. Place a plate or cutting board on top of the wrapped tofu and press gently to squeeze out more moisture. Let it sit for about 15-20 minutes to remove excess water.
2. **Cut and marinate the tofu:**
    - Cut the pressed tofu into cubes or rectangles, about 1-inch in size. In a shallow dish or bowl, whisk together soy sauce, mirin (or rice vinegar), honey (or maple syrup), sesame oil, minced garlic, and grated ginger. Add the tofu cubes to the marinade and gently toss to coat. Let it marinate for at least 15-20 minutes, or longer if time allows, flipping the tofu cubes occasionally to ensure even marination.
3. **Make the teriyaki sauce:**
    - In a small bowl, whisk together water and cornstarch (or arrowroot powder) until dissolved. Set aside.
4. **Cook the tofu:**
    - Heat vegetable oil in a large skillet or non-stick pan over medium-high heat. Once hot, add the marinated tofu cubes in a single layer (reserve the marinade). Cook the tofu for about 4-5 minutes on each side, or until golden and crispy. Be gentle when flipping to avoid breaking the tofu cubes. Remove the tofu from the skillet and set aside.
5. **Simmer the sauce:**
    - Lower the heat to medium. Pour the reserved marinade into the skillet. Bring it to a simmer, stirring frequently. Cook for 1-2 minutes until the sauce thickens slightly.
6. **Combine tofu and sauce:**

- Return the cooked tofu to the skillet with the thickened teriyaki sauce. Gently toss the tofu cubes in the sauce until evenly coated. Cook for another 1-2 minutes, allowing the tofu to absorb the flavors of the sauce.
7. **Serve:**
    - Transfer the teriyaki tofu to a serving dish. Garnish with sesame seeds and sliced green onions if desired.
8. **Enjoy:**
    - Serve teriyaki tofu hot over steamed rice or noodles. It pairs well with a side of stir-fried vegetables or a fresh salad.

Tips:

- **Crispy tofu:** For extra crispy tofu, ensure the skillet is hot before adding the tofu cubes, and avoid overcrowding the pan.
- **Gluten-free option:** Use tamari instead of soy sauce to make the recipe gluten-free.
- **Variations:** Add diced bell peppers, broccoli florets, or snap peas to the skillet along with the tofu for a more substantial dish.
- **Storage:** Leftover teriyaki tofu can be stored in an airtight container in the refrigerator for up to 3 days. Reheat gently in a skillet or microwave before serving.

Teriyaki tofu is a versatile and delicious vegetarian dish that's sure to satisfy your taste buds with its sweet and savory flavors. Enjoy this homemade teriyaki tofu as a tasty and wholesome meal!

Broccoli Salad

Ingredients:

- 4 cups broccoli florets (about 1 medium head of broccoli)
- 1/2 cup red onion, finely chopped
- 1/2 cup raisins or dried cranberries
- 1/2 cup sunflower seeds or sliced almonds
- 1/2 cup mayonnaise
- 2 tablespoons apple cider vinegar
- 1 tablespoon honey or maple syrup
- Salt and pepper, to taste

Instructions:

1. **Prepare the broccoli:**
    - Wash the broccoli thoroughly and cut it into bite-sized florets. If desired, you can blanch the broccoli florets in boiling water for 1-2 minutes, then immediately transfer them to ice water to stop the cooking process. This step is optional and helps to retain the vibrant green color.
2. **Make the dressing:**
    - In a small bowl, whisk together mayonnaise, apple cider vinegar, honey (or maple syrup), salt, and pepper until smooth and well combined.
3. **Assemble the salad:**
    - In a large mixing bowl, combine the broccoli florets, chopped red onion, raisins (or dried cranberries), and sunflower seeds (or sliced almonds).
4. **Add the dressing:**
    - Pour the dressing over the broccoli mixture. Toss gently to coat all the ingredients evenly with the dressing.
5. **Chill and marinate (optional):**
    - Cover the bowl with plastic wrap or transfer the salad to an airtight container. Refrigerate for at least 1 hour, or overnight, to allow the flavors to meld together.
6. **Serve:**
    - Before serving, give the broccoli salad a final toss. Taste and adjust seasoning if needed. Optionally, sprinkle additional sunflower seeds or sliced almonds on top for extra crunch.

Tips:

- **Variations:** You can customize your broccoli salad by adding other ingredients like crispy bacon, shredded cheddar cheese, diced apples, or chopped celery.
- **Make it vegan:** Substitute mayonnaise with vegan mayonnaise or a combination of vegan yogurt and olive oil.

- **Storage:** Leftover broccoli salad can be stored in an airtight container in the refrigerator for up to 3 days. Stir well before serving.

Broccoli salad is a versatile and delicious side dish that complements any meal. It's perfect for potlucks, barbecues, or as a healthy lunch option. Enjoy the crisp texture and vibrant flavors of this classic broccoli salad!

Pulled Pork Sandwiches

Ingredients for Pulled Pork:

- 3-4 pounds pork shoulder (also known as pork butt), boneless
- 1 tablespoon brown sugar
- 1 tablespoon smoked paprika
- 1 tablespoon garlic powder
- 1 tablespoon onion powder
- 1 tablespoon chili powder
- 1 tablespoon ground cumin
- 1 tablespoon salt
- 1 teaspoon black pepper
- 1 cup chicken or vegetable broth
- 1 cup barbecue sauce (homemade or store-bought)
- Hamburger buns or sandwich rolls, for serving

Instructions:

1. **Prepare the pork shoulder:**
    - In a small bowl, mix together brown sugar, smoked paprika, garlic powder, onion powder, chili powder, cumin, salt, and black pepper to create a dry rub.
    - Rub the dry rub all over the pork shoulder, covering it evenly. Let it sit at room temperature for about 30 minutes to allow the flavors to penetrate the meat.
2. **Cook the pork shoulder:**
    - Preheat your oven to 300°F (150°C).
    - Place the seasoned pork shoulder in a roasting pan or Dutch oven. Pour chicken or vegetable broth around the pork (not over it). Cover tightly with aluminum foil or the lid of the Dutch oven.
    - Roast in the preheated oven for about 4-5 hours, or until the pork is very tender and easily pulls apart with a fork.
3. **Shred the pork:**
    - Remove the pork shoulder from the oven. Using two forks, shred the meat directly in the roasting pan. Discard any large pieces of fat.
4. **Add barbecue sauce:**
    - Pour barbecue sauce over the shredded pork and stir to combine, ensuring the pork is evenly coated with the sauce. If you prefer a saucier sandwich, you can add more barbecue sauce to taste.
5. **Assemble the sandwiches:**
    - Toast the hamburger buns or sandwich rolls lightly, if desired. Spoon a generous amount of pulled pork onto the bottom half of each bun. Top with the other half of the bun.
6. **Serve:**

- Serve the pulled pork sandwiches immediately while warm. You can serve them with coleslaw, pickles, or additional barbecue sauce on the side.

Homemade Barbecue Sauce (Optional):

If you'd like to make your own barbecue sauce, here's a simple recipe:

- 1 cup ketchup
- 1/2 cup apple cider vinegar
- 1/4 cup brown sugar
- 2 tablespoons Worcestershire sauce
- 1 tablespoon Dijon mustard
- 1 teaspoon smoked paprika
- 1 teaspoon garlic powder
- 1/2 teaspoon onion powder
- Salt and pepper, to taste

Instructions for Barbecue Sauce:

1. In a medium saucepan, combine all ingredients over medium heat.
2. Bring to a simmer, stirring occasionally.
3. Reduce heat to low and let simmer for 15-20 minutes, stirring occasionally, until the sauce has thickened slightly.
4. Remove from heat and let cool before using. Store any leftover barbecue sauce in the refrigerator for up to 1 week.

Enjoy these delicious pulled pork sandwiches with tender, flavorful pork and your favorite barbecue sauce for a satisfying meal!

Pasta with Garlic Butter Sauce

Ingredients:

- 8 ounces (225g) pasta (such as spaghetti, fettuccine, or linguine)
- 4 tablespoons unsalted butter
- 4 cloves garlic, minced
- 1/4 teaspoon red pepper flakes (optional, for a hint of heat)
- Salt and pepper, to taste
- Grated Parmesan cheese, for serving
- Fresh parsley, chopped, for garnish (optional)

Instructions:

1. **Cook the pasta:**
    - Bring a large pot of salted water to a boil. Cook the pasta according to package instructions until al dente. Reserve about 1/2 cup of pasta cooking water, then drain the pasta.
2. **Make the garlic butter sauce:**
    - In a large skillet or frying pan, melt the butter over medium heat. Add the minced garlic and red pepper flakes (if using). Sauté for about 1-2 minutes, stirring constantly, until the garlic is fragrant and just starting to turn golden. Be careful not to burn the garlic.
3. **Combine pasta and sauce:**
    - Add the cooked and drained pasta to the skillet with the garlic butter sauce. Toss gently to coat the pasta evenly with the sauce. If the pasta seems dry, add a splash of the reserved pasta cooking water to loosen it up.
4. **Season and serve:**
    - Season the pasta with salt and pepper to taste. Sprinkle grated Parmesan cheese over the pasta and toss again to combine.
5. **Garnish and enjoy:**
    - Transfer the pasta to serving plates or a large serving dish. Garnish with chopped fresh parsley if desired. Serve immediately, with extra Parmesan cheese on the side if desired.

Tips:

- **Variations:** You can add sautéed shrimp, grilled chicken, or roasted vegetables to the pasta for added protein and flavor.
- **Garlic:** Adjust the amount of garlic to suit your taste preferences. You can use more or less depending on how garlicky you like your dish.
- **Herbs:** Besides parsley, you can use chopped fresh basil or thyme for a different flavor profile.

- **Storage:** Leftover pasta with garlic butter sauce can be stored in an airtight container in the refrigerator for up to 3 days. Reheat gently in a skillet with a splash of water or broth to prevent drying out.

Pasta with garlic butter sauce is a quick and satisfying dish that's perfect for busy weeknights or whenever you crave a simple yet flavorful meal. Enjoy the rich buttery garlic sauce coating every strand of pasta!

Quiche

Ingredients:

For the pastry crust:

- 1 1/4 cups all-purpose flour
- 1/2 teaspoon salt
- 1/2 cup unsalted butter, chilled and diced
- 1/4 cup ice water

For the quiche filling:

- 1 tablespoon olive oil or butter
- 1 small onion, finely chopped
- 1 cup diced cooked ham, bacon, or cooked vegetables (such as spinach, mushrooms, or broccoli)
- 1 cup shredded cheese (such as cheddar, Gruyère, or Swiss)
- 4 large eggs
- 1 cup milk or half-and-half
- Salt and pepper, to taste
- Pinch of nutmeg (optional)

Instructions:

For the pastry crust:

1. **Prepare the pastry crust:**
    - In a large bowl, combine the flour and salt. Cut in the chilled butter using a pastry cutter or fork until the mixture resembles coarse crumbs.
    - Gradually add the ice water, a tablespoon at a time, tossing with a fork until the dough comes together. Be careful not to overwork the dough.
    - Shape the dough into a disk, wrap it in plastic wrap, and refrigerate for at least 1 hour (or up to overnight).
2. **Preheat the oven:**
    - Preheat your oven to 375°F (190°C).
3. **Roll out and line the pie dish:**
    - On a lightly floured surface, roll out the chilled dough into a circle slightly larger than your pie dish. Carefully transfer the dough to a 9-inch pie dish. Press the dough gently into the bottom and sides of the dish. Trim any excess dough and crimp the edges.
4. **Blind bake the crust (optional):**
    - Line the pie crust with parchment paper or aluminum foil and fill it with pie weights, dried beans, or rice to prevent it from puffing up during baking. Bake for 15 minutes. Remove the weights and parchment paper/foil, then bake for an

additional 5 minutes until the crust is lightly golden. Remove from the oven and set aside.

For the quiche filling:

1. **Prepare the filling:**
    - In a medium skillet, heat olive oil or butter over medium heat. Add the chopped onion and cook until softened and translucent, about 5 minutes. Add the diced ham, bacon, or cooked vegetables and cook for another 2-3 minutes. Remove from heat and let cool slightly.
2. **Assemble the quiche:**
    - Sprinkle half of the shredded cheese evenly over the bottom of the pre-baked pie crust. Spread the cooked onion and ham mixture (or vegetables) over the cheese. Sprinkle the remaining cheese on top.
3. **Make the custard mixture:**
    - In a bowl, whisk together eggs, milk or half-and-half, salt, pepper, and nutmeg (if using) until well combined.
4. **Bake the quiche:**
    - Pour the egg mixture evenly over the filling in the pie crust. Place the quiche on a baking sheet (to catch any spills) and carefully transfer it to the preheated oven.
    - Bake for 35-40 minutes, or until the quiche is set and the top is golden brown. It should jiggle slightly in the center but not be liquidy.
5. **Cool and serve:**
    - Remove the quiche from the oven and let it cool for 10 minutes before slicing and serving. Garnish with fresh herbs if desired.

Tips:

- **Variations:** You can customize your quiche by using different cheeses, adding herbs like parsley or thyme, or incorporating other fillings such as cooked sausage, smoked salmon, or roasted vegetables.
- **Make ahead:** Quiche can be prepared ahead of time. Bake it fully, let it cool completely, then cover and refrigerate. Reheat slices in the oven or microwave before serving.
- **Serve suggestions:** Quiche is delicious served warm or at room temperature. It pairs well with a side salad dressed with vinaigrette for a complete meal.

Quiche is versatile, satisfying, and perfect for brunches, lunches, or light dinners. Enjoy this classic dish with your favorite fillings and flavors!

Asian Slaw

Ingredients:

For the slaw:

- 4 cups shredded cabbage (green cabbage or Napa cabbage)
- 1 cup shredded carrots
- 1 red bell pepper, thinly sliced
- 1/2 cup thinly sliced red onion
- 1/4 cup chopped fresh cilantro
- 1/4 cup chopped fresh mint
- 1/4 cup chopped roasted peanuts or sliced almonds (optional, for garnish)
- 1 tablespoon sesame seeds (optional, for garnish)

For the dressing:

- 1/4 cup rice vinegar
- 2 tablespoons soy sauce (or tamari for gluten-free)
- 1 tablespoon honey or maple syrup
- 1 tablespoon sesame oil
- 1 tablespoon freshly grated ginger
- 1 clove garlic, minced
- 1/2 teaspoon sriracha or chili garlic sauce (optional, for a bit of heat)
- Salt and pepper, to taste

Instructions:

1. **Prepare the vegetables:**
   - In a large bowl, combine shredded cabbage, shredded carrots, sliced red bell pepper, sliced red onion, chopped cilantro, and chopped mint. Toss to mix evenly.
2. **Make the dressing:**
   - In a small bowl, whisk together rice vinegar, soy sauce, honey (or maple syrup), sesame oil, grated ginger, minced garlic, sriracha (or chili garlic sauce), salt, and pepper until well combined.
3. **Combine slaw and dressing:**
   - Pour the dressing over the prepared vegetables. Toss the slaw gently to coat all the vegetables with the dressing. Adjust seasoning to taste, adding more salt or pepper if needed.
4. **Chill and marinate (optional):**
   - Cover the bowl with plastic wrap or transfer the slaw to an airtight container. Refrigerate for at least 30 minutes to allow the flavors to meld together.
5. **Serve:**
   - Before serving, toss the Asian slaw again to mix the dressing evenly. Garnish with chopped roasted peanuts or sliced almonds, and sesame seeds if desired.

Tips:

- **Variations:** You can add additional ingredients to the slaw such as shredded broccoli, snap peas, or sliced cucumber for extra crunch and flavor.
- **Make it ahead:** Asian slaw can be made ahead of time and stored in the refrigerator for up to 2 days. The flavors will continue to meld together, making it even more delicious.
- **Serve suggestions:** Asian slaw is great as a side dish or as a topping for sandwiches, tacos, or wraps. It pairs well with grilled chicken, shrimp, or tofu.

This Asian slaw recipe is refreshing, crunchy, and packed with vibrant flavors. It's perfect for summer picnics, potlucks, or as a healthy side dish any time of the year. Enjoy the delicious blend of vegetables and zesty dressing!

Baked Salmon

Ingredients:

- 4 salmon fillets (about 6 ounces each), skin-on or skinless
- Salt and pepper, to taste
- 2 tablespoons olive oil or melted butter
- 2 cloves garlic, minced (optional)
- 1 lemon, sliced into rounds or wedges
- Fresh herbs (such as dill, parsley, or thyme), for garnish

Instructions:

1. **Preheat the oven:**
   - Preheat your oven to 375°F (190°C). Line a baking sheet with parchment paper or lightly grease it with oil or cooking spray.
2. **Prepare the salmon:**
   - Pat the salmon fillets dry with paper towels. This helps the salmon to cook evenly and ensures a nice sear or crust.
3. **Season the salmon:**
   - Place the salmon fillets skin-side down (if using skin-on) on the prepared baking sheet. Season both sides of the salmon with salt and pepper to taste. Drizzle olive oil or melted butter over the salmon fillets. Rub minced garlic over the tops of the fillets, if desired.
4. **Bake the salmon:**
   - Arrange lemon slices or wedges on top of the salmon fillets. Bake in the preheated oven for 12-15 minutes, depending on the thickness of your salmon fillets. The salmon is done when it flakes easily with a fork and reaches an internal temperature of 145°F (63°C).
5. **Garnish and serve:**
   - Once baked, remove the salmon from the oven and garnish with fresh herbs, such as dill, parsley, or thyme. Serve the baked salmon hot with additional lemon wedges on the side.

Tips for Perfect Baked Salmon:

- **Skin-on or skinless:** You can bake salmon with or without the skin. If using skin-on, the skin helps to keep the fish moist. If you prefer skinless fillets, that works just as well.
- **Flavor variations:** Experiment with different herbs and seasonings. Besides garlic, you can use smoked paprika, lemon pepper, or a sprinkle of your favorite seasoning blend.
- **Cooking time:** Adjust baking time based on the thickness of your salmon fillets. Thicker fillets may require a few extra minutes in the oven.
- **Serving suggestions:** Baked salmon pairs well with a variety of side dishes such as roasted vegetables, steamed asparagus, quinoa, or a fresh green salad.

Baked salmon is a versatile dish that's perfect for any occasion, from weeknight dinners to special gatherings. Enjoy the tender, flaky texture and delicious flavor of this simple and healthy meal!

Rice and Beans

Ingredients:

- 1 cup long-grain white rice (such as jasmine or basmati)
- 1 can (15 ounces) black beans, drained and rinsed (or about 1 1/2 cups cooked black beans)
- 1 small onion, finely chopped
- 2 cloves garlic, minced
- 1 bell pepper (any color), diced
- 1 tablespoon olive oil
- 1 teaspoon ground cumin
- 1/2 teaspoon chili powder (adjust to taste)
- Salt and pepper, to taste
- 2 cups vegetable broth or water
- Fresh cilantro or parsley, chopped (for garnish, optional)
- Lime wedges, for serving (optional)

Instructions:

1. **Prepare the rice:**
   - Rinse the rice under cold water until the water runs clear. This removes excess starch and helps prevent the rice from becoming too sticky.
   - In a large skillet or pot, heat the olive oil over medium heat. Add the chopped onion and bell pepper. Cook for 3-4 minutes until they begin to soften.
2. **Add garlic and spices:**
   - Add the minced garlic, ground cumin, and chili powder to the skillet. Cook for another 1-2 minutes until fragrant, stirring constantly to prevent burning.
3. **Combine rice and beans:**
   - Add the rinsed rice to the skillet and stir to coat it with the onion, pepper, and spices. Cook for about 1 minute to toast the rice slightly.
4. **Cook with broth:**
   - Pour in the vegetable broth or water. Season with salt and pepper to taste. Bring the mixture to a boil, then reduce the heat to low. Cover and simmer for 15-20 minutes, or until the rice is tender and the liquid is absorbed.
5. **Add beans:**
   - Once the rice is cooked, stir in the drained and rinsed black beans. Cover the skillet and let it sit for a few minutes to allow the beans to heat through.
6. **Serve:**
   - Fluff the rice and beans mixture with a fork. Taste and adjust seasoning if needed. Garnish with chopped cilantro or parsley if desired. Serve hot, with lime wedges on the side for squeezing over the dish.

Tips for Making Rice and Beans:

- **Variations:** Feel free to customize the dish by using different types of beans such as kidney beans or pinto beans. You can also add diced tomatoes, corn, or a splash of hot sauce for added flavor.
- **Protein:** To make it a complete meal, serve rice and beans with a side of grilled chicken, shrimp, or tofu.
- **Storage:** Leftovers can be stored in an airtight container in the refrigerator for up to 3 days. Reheat gently in the microwave or on the stovetop with a splash of water or broth to refresh the rice.
- **Nutrition:** Rice and beans together provide a good balance of carbohydrates, protein, and fiber. It's a budget-friendly and filling dish suitable for vegetarian and vegan diets.

Rice and beans is not only delicious and comforting but also versatile and easy to prepare. Enjoy this wholesome dish as a main course or a side dish with your favorite toppings and accompaniments!

Stuffed Zucchini Boats

Ingredients:

- 4 medium zucchini
- 1 tablespoon olive oil
- 1 small onion, finely chopped
- 2 cloves garlic, minced
- 1 bell pepper (any color), diced
- 1 cup diced tomatoes (fresh or canned)
- 1 cup cooked quinoa or rice
- 1 cup cooked and drained black beans (or any beans of your choice)
- 1 teaspoon dried oregano
- 1 teaspoon dried basil
- Salt and pepper, to taste
- 1/2 cup shredded cheese (such as mozzarella, cheddar, or Parmesan)
- Fresh parsley or cilantro, chopped, for garnish (optional)

Instructions:

1. **Prepare the zucchini:**
    - Preheat your oven to 400°F (200°C). Line a baking sheet with parchment paper.
    - Wash the zucchini and trim off the ends. Slice each zucchini in half lengthwise. Use a spoon to carefully scoop out the flesh from the center of each half, leaving about a 1/4-inch border around the edges. Reserve the zucchini flesh for later use.
2. **Prepare the filling:**
    - In a large skillet, heat olive oil over medium heat. Add the chopped onion and cook until softened, about 3-4 minutes. Add the minced garlic and diced bell pepper. Cook for another 2-3 minutes until the peppers start to soften.
3. **Combine filling ingredients:**
    - Chop the reserved zucchini flesh and add it to the skillet with the onion and bell pepper mixture. Cook for 2-3 minutes until the zucchini is tender.
    - Add the diced tomatoes, cooked quinoa or rice, cooked black beans, dried oregano, dried basil, salt, and pepper to the skillet. Stir everything together and cook for another 2-3 minutes until heated through. Taste and adjust seasoning if needed.
4. **Assemble the zucchini boats:**
    - Place the hollowed-out zucchini halves on the prepared baking sheet. Spoon the filling mixture evenly into each zucchini boat, pressing down gently to pack the filling.
5. **Bake the stuffed zucchini:**
    - Cover the baking sheet with foil and bake in the preheated oven for 20-25 minutes, or until the zucchini is tender when pierced with a fork.

6. **Add cheese and finish baking:**
   - Remove the foil from the baking sheet. Sprinkle shredded cheese over each stuffed zucchini boat. Return the baking sheet to the oven and bake uncovered for an additional 5-10 minutes, or until the cheese is melted and bubbly.
7. **Garnish and serve:**
   - Remove the stuffed zucchini boats from the oven. Garnish with chopped fresh parsley or cilantro if desired. Serve hot as a main dish or a hearty side dish.

Tips for Stuffed Zucchini Boats:

- **Variations:** You can customize the filling by adding ground meat, diced chicken, or other vegetables like corn, spinach, or mushrooms.
- **Make ahead:** You can prepare the filling ahead of time and store it in the refrigerator. When ready to serve, assemble the zucchini boats and bake them.
- **Gluten-free option:** Use cooked quinoa or gluten-free rice for a gluten-free version of this dish.
- **Leftovers:** Stuffed zucchini boats are great for leftovers. Store them in an airtight container in the refrigerator for up to 3 days and reheat gently in the oven or microwave before serving.

Stuffed zucchini boats are a nutritious and satisfying dish that's perfect for a wholesome meal. Enjoy the combination of tender zucchini, flavorful filling, and melted cheese in every bite!

Avocado Toast

Ingredients:

- 2 slices of whole grain bread (or bread of your choice)
- 1 ripe avocado
- Salt and pepper, to taste
- Red pepper flakes (optional, for a bit of heat)
- Lemon juice (optional, to prevent avocado from browning)
- Toasted sesame seeds or everything bagel seasoning (optional, for garnish)

Instructions:

1. **Prepare the avocado:**
   - Cut the ripe avocado in half lengthwise. Remove the pit and scoop the flesh into a bowl using a spoon.
2. **Mash the avocado:**
   - Mash the avocado with a fork until smooth or chunky, depending on your preference. If desired, add a splash of lemon juice to prevent the avocado from browning.
3. **Toast the bread:**
   - Toast the slices of bread until golden brown and crispy.
4. **Assemble avocado toast:**
   - Spread the mashed avocado evenly onto the toasted bread slices.
5. **Season and garnish:**
   - Sprinkle salt and pepper over the avocado toast to taste. Add a pinch of red pepper flakes for some heat, if desired.
   - Optionally, garnish with toasted sesame seeds or everything bagel seasoning for extra flavor and texture.
6. **Serve:**
   - Serve the avocado toast immediately while the bread is still warm and crispy.

Variations:

- **Egg on top:** Fry or poach an egg and place it on top of the avocado toast for added protein and richness.
- **Tomato and basil:** Add slices of fresh tomato and sprinkle with chopped fresh basil for a refreshing twist.
- **Smoked salmon:** Top avocado toast with smoked salmon slices and a squeeze of lemon juice for a luxurious flavor.
- **Cucumber and radish:** Thinly slice cucumber and radish and layer them over the avocado for a crunchy texture.
- **Balsamic glaze:** Drizzle a balsamic glaze or reduction over the avocado toast for a sweet and tangy flavor.

- **Goat cheese:** Spread a layer of creamy goat cheese on the toast before adding the mashed avocado for a tangy contrast.

Tips:

- **Choosing ripe avocados:** Look for avocados that yield slightly to gentle pressure when squeezed. They should be firm but give a little.
- **Customize to taste:** Avocado toast is highly customizable based on your preferences. Experiment with different toppings, seasonings, and types of bread to create your favorite combinations.
- **Nutritional boost:** For added nutrition, sprinkle with chia seeds, hemp seeds, or nutritional yeast over the avocado.

Avocado toast is not only delicious but also nutritious, providing healthy fats, fiber, and vitamins. Enjoy it for breakfast, lunch, or as a quick snack any time of the day!